Anchored for the Storm

ANCHORED
for the Storm

*Devotions for Caregivers
Drawing Strength from God*

Donn King

HIDDEN MENTOR MEDIA
Maryville, TN

Hidden Mentor
MEDIA

ISBN-13: 978-1-969835-06-3 (ebook)
ISBN-13: 978-1-969835-07-0 (paperback)

Hidden Mentor Media

For Hannah,
and through her, for caregivers everywhere.

Contents

Foreword

Roughly fifty million people serve as unpaid caregivers in the United States at any given moment. Fifty million people who have arranged their lives—their sleep, their schedules, their ambitions, their relationships—around the needs of someone who depends on them. And that number does not capture everyone this book is for.

It does not count the parents whose creative and professional lives are perpetually interrupted by the demands of raising small children. It does not count the people managing chronic illness or disability of their own who find that life rarely proceeds on their preferred terms. It does not count everyone who has found themselves in a season not of their choosing, tending something or someone that cannot wait. If you are any of those people, Donn King has written this book for you.

He has earned the right.

For more than two decades, Donn and his wife Janet cared for their daughter Hannah, who had been severely disabled from birth and was dependent on a ventilator for her life. Then Janet herself became disabled and wheelchair-bound. Donn has lived, for an extended stretch, in a situation of layered caregiving complexity that most of us can barely imagine, and he has done it while continuing to write, to teach, to think, and to stay grounded in faith.

Donn will tell you in his introduction, but I must share a sad fact here: Hannah died on December 15, 2025.

My wife Sally and I attended her memorial service. I want to say something about that gathering. The number of people was modest, but the diversity of the room was remarkable — people from many different places and walks of life, drawn together by their connection to Donn and Janet over years of a life lived with unusual openness. It was the kind of gathering that tells you something true about the people at the center of it. Donn and Janet did not retreat behind their circumstances. They built something — friendships, community, a presence in the world — in the middle of everything that could have made that impossible.

This book is part of what they built.

Anchored for the Storm is a companion to Donn's earlier book, *Creating While Caring*, which addressed the particular challenges facing people who feel called to create — to write, paint, compose, make — but whose caregiving lives make sustained creative work enormously difficult. That book was sympathetic, practical, and ultimately spiritual. It changed the way I think about my own creative work and what it means to pursue it faithfully under constraint. I wrote at the time that it was an absolutely terrific book, and I stand by that.

This book goes deeper. Where *Creating While Caring* addresses what caregivers do with their creative and professional energy, *Anchored for the Storm* addresses what sustains them at the root. It is a book of devotions — daily companionship for people in the long middle of a caregiving life — and it is unlike much devotional writing I have encountered.

The difference is honesty.

Most devotional writing for caregivers falls into one of two patterns. The first softens the reality. It acknowledges difficulty in general terms before moving quickly toward reassurance and resolution. The second offers theological substance, but at a distance, as though faith were a set of propositions to affirm rather than a living relationship to inhabit in the hardest hours. Donn does neither. He names things plainly. Exhaustion. Grief. The slow accumulation of losses that never get announced. The quiet resentment that coexists with genuine love. The nights that seem to have no end.

And then, without pretending those things aren't real, he points to a God who is already present in them.

That is the word this kind of book must deliver: not that God will rescue you from the hard season, but that God is with you inside it. Donn grounds this claim not in sentiment but in Scripture, read carefully, read in context, read with the honesty of someone who has needed it to be true and tested it against real experience. When he takes you to Isaiah 40, he places you in Babylonian exile first, so the promise of renewed strength lands where it belongs. When he opens Lamentations, he does not rush past the devastation to arrive at the mercy. He lets you stand in both. That is not merely good biblical scholarship. It is pastoral care.

One final thought. Donn wrote most of these devotions while Hannah was still alive. Some he wrote while she was hospitalized—while outcomes were uncertain and decisions were still being made. Donn wrote from inside the difficulty, not safely in retrospect. That willingness gives these pages a quality that cannot be manufactured after the fact. You are not reading someone who has arrived and is looking back. You are reading someone who chose, in the midst of the walking, to look up.

Now Hannah is gone. The caregiving season that shaped so much of Donn and Janet's life has ended. And what I can tell you, having known Donn through those years and having stood in that memorial service, is that the faith he describes in these pages is real. It held. Not because the road was easy, or because every prayer was answered as hoped, or because the grief was somehow bypassed. It held because the God he writes about is who he says he is.

If you are a caregiver, or if you are simply someone whose life is not proceeding on your preferred terms (which is most of us eventually), this book was written for you. Read it slowly. Carry it with you. Return to it when the night is long.

It was written by someone who knows what that night feels like.

And it points, reliably, to the light.

—Jim Stovall
Author of the "Nathan Tower series"

Introduction

At four o'clock one morning my daughter's oxygen level dropped, and the pulse-ox alarm shattered the quiet of the ICU.

I jumped up from the hard chair beside her bed.

For years I had lived with a strange nighttime rhythm: sleep two or three hours, wake up, give medicine, clear her airway, try to sleep again. I had repeated that routine hundreds of times.

This time the routine failed.

I tried to clear Hannah's tracheostomy with the suction tube, something I had done thousands of times before.

The airway wouldn't clear. Her oxygen kept dropping. I realized I needed to perform an emergency trach change.

At home I knew exactly where every piece of equipment lived. In this ICU I didn't. I pressed the nurse call button and began searching for supplies while the alarm screamed louder and louder.

A nurse hurried in, but she had never handled this situation before. I needed a ten-milliliter syringe to collapse the small balloon that held the trach tube in place. Without collapsing that balloon I couldn't safely remove the tube.

Several pre-filled syringes sat nearby, already loaded with sterile saline. I grabbed one, squirted the saline onto the floor, and used the syringe to collapse the balloon.

The old trach came out.

I inserted the replacement.

Oxygen began flowing into my daughter's lungs again.

Hours later, still shaky from adrenaline and short on sleep, I sat beside her bed and watched her chest slowly rise and fall.

And questions filled my mind.

How much longer can I keep doing this?

What would have happened if I hadn't been here?

What will happen when I can no longer sleep beside her bed?

That night didn't stand alone.

Hannah spent much of her life in hospitals. She experienced more than forty hospitalizations, and we eventually lost count of the emergency room visits. My wife lives with partial disability, so I usually stayed with Hannah during those hospital nights.

The dim lights.

The steady beeping of the pulse oximeter.

The regular inflation of the blood pressure cuff.

Respiratory therapists moving quietly through the halls.

The sounds from nearby rooms where other children faced their own medical struggles.

After a while those nights blurred together.

Caregiving carries a complicated mix of emotions.

Fatigue.

Anxiety.

Moments of joy when something finally works.

Frustration.

Anger at a medical system that sometimes feels impossibly complicated.

Deep gratitude for doctors and nurses who serve with extraordinary dedication.

Isolation.

And questions for God.

If you are reading this book, chances are that you—or someone you love—serves as a caregiver. And if you picked up a devotional book, you probably believe in God.

That combination stretches both body and faith.

You may have opened this book hoping someone will finally explain why these things happen.

I can't offer that explanation.

What I can offer comes from walking a similar road through the same country.

As I wrote these devotionals, Hannah still lived. Many of the reflections in these pages grew out of nights like the one I just described—long hospital hours, quiet prayers, and small moments of grace in difficult circumstances.

Before I finished this book, however, Hannah's life on this earth came to an end.

Her death changed many things.

I no longer serve as a caregiver in the same way I once did, though I still care for my wife in the ways her disability requires. The daily routines have changed, but the memories, the love, and the questions remain.

So as you read these pages, you will sometimes encounter Hannah as if she still sits beside me.

I chose not to rewrite those moments.

They tell the story honestly as it unfolded while I lived it.

Over the years I learned something important: much of life remains beyond human understanding. In that sense we humans resemble my old dog.

My dog used to watch with deep concern when her humans rushed around the house in the morning—gulping coffee, grabbing a briefcase, running out the door, running back in for the car keys, then rushing out again. No explanation could help her understand the concept of getting to work on time.

She also couldn't understand why I allowed a woman in a white coat to stick a sharp needle into her leg—sometimes even helping hold her still while it happened.

Yet afterward she still trusted me. She would lick my hand, even while suffering the needle.

Much about this world escapes my understanding.

I don't understand why evil exists. I don't understand why suffering strikes some lives with such force. I don't understand how my daughter's profound disabilities fit within the vast design of the universe.

But I have learned something else.

Trust doesn't require complete understanding.

Some scholars believe the Book of Job may stand as the oldest book in the Bible. If that is true, people have wrestled with suffering and faith for as long as humans have written about God.

When God finally answered Job, he didn't offer a tidy explanation. Instead, he revealed the vastness of creation and the limits of human understanding.

The message didn't dismiss Job's suffering. It reminded him that the universe stretches far beyond what any human mind can grasp.

Christians believe God responded to that problem in a remarkable way. Instead of explaining suffering from a distance, God entered human life Himself in the Incarnation.

God came to live among us. God shared our pain. And God assured us that we would never face life alone.

This book can't solve your problems.

But perhaps it can sit beside you for a while.

In the hospital chair.
In the waiting room.
In the long night at home.

That kind of companionship helped me.
I hope these pages do the same for you.

How to Use This Book

Caregiving rarely runs on a predictable schedule.

Some days move along quietly. Other days feel like a medical drama, a logistical puzzle, and an emotional roller coaster all happening before lunch. In a life like that, a devotional that expects you to show up at the same time every day and follow a carefully planned reading schedule may not be very helpful.

So this book does not work that way.

The devotionals in these pages are **not dated** and **not arranged in sections**. You can open the book almost anywhere and find a short reflection, a passage of Scripture, and a prayer meant to meet you in that moment.

Some readers may choose to read one each day. Others may pick up the book only when a difficult day arrives and they need a few minutes of encouragement. Either approach is perfectly fine.

You can also make use of the **topic index in the back of the book**. Caregiving has a way of bringing certain challenges to the surface again and again—fatigue, frustration, guilt, fear, gratitude, hope, and sometimes the quiet question of whether you are doing enough.

If something specific weighs on your heart, the index can help you find devotionals that speak directly to that situation.

However you use this book, remember one thing: these pages are not meant to place another demand on your already full life. They are meant to offer a small pause—a moment to breathe, to remember that God is present, and to receive a little strength for whatever comes next.

Read a little. Reflect a little. Pray if you can.

And if all you manage some days is a single sentence that reminds you that you are not alone, that will be enough

Stay in touch

Caregiving can feel lonely, even when we are surrounded by people. If this book encouraged you, I'd love to stay connected. By scanning the QR code or visiting

DonnKing.com/AnchorConnect

you can share a little about your caregiving journey, request prayer if you wish, and choose whether you'd like occasional encouragement and updates about future resources. There's no obligation, no pressure, and you can unsubscribe at any time. My hope is simply to continue offering support to caregivers who are walking through difficult seasons together..

When the World Falls Apart

God is our refuge and strength,
a help always near in times of great trouble.
That's why we won't be afraid when the world falls apart,
when the mountains crumble into the center of the sea,
when its waters roar and rage,
when the mountains shake because of its surging waves.

Psalm 46:1–3

Martin Luther found in this psalm the foundation for *A Mighty Fortress Is Our God*. He lived through plague, political upheaval, and fierce personal battles, yet he leaned on the words of the Korahite singers: "God is our refuge and strength." For Luther, the psalm became a battle cry of faith in the midst of danger, a reminder that God had not abandoned him even when the world seemed to collapse.

As caregivers, we know that feeling. One medical crisis, one sleepless night, one abrupt shift in routine, and the whole structure of our lives can feel as if it's caving in. *The Message* paraphrases it powerfully: "We stand fearless at the cliff-edge of doom, courageous in seastorm and earthquake." That's exactly where caregiving often puts us—at the edge, barely holding on, staring at the waves. And yet, the psalmist insists: "God is a safe place to hide, ready to help when we need him."

This psalm has been a song of courage in crisis for centuries, and it can be for us, too. In those moments when chaos presses hardest, you don't need the whole psalm. Just a phrase. Whisper it, pray it, cling to it. "God is our refuge and strength." Or, "Jacob-wrestling God fights for us." (Remember—*us* means you and the one for whom you care.) Or simply: "God is a safe place to hide." Even a handful of words can anchor you when the storm rages loudest.

Prayer

Father, when the ground shakes beneath me and the waves roar around me, remind me that you are my refuge and strength. Let these words sink deep enough to rise up when I need them most. Keep me steady in the storm. Amen.

Journaling Prompt

What short phrase from Psalm 46 can you carry with you and repeat in moments of crisis to remind you that God is your safe place?

A Season You Didn't Choose

There's a season for everything and a time for every matter under heaven.

Ecclesiastes 3:1

Ecclesiastes is often misunderstood as either pessimistic or poetic comfort. In truth, it is unsentimental wisdom. Traditionally associated with Solomon, Ecclesiastes doesn't rush to reassure. It observes life as it is, naming its limits, contradictions, and unanswered questions. Chapter 3 belongs to a larger reflection on time, not as something we control, but as something we inhabit.

When Ecclesiastes says there is "a season for everything," it isn't saying every season is pleasant or evenly distributed. The list that follows includes birth and death, tearing down and building up, weeping and laughing. These seasons don't arrive by vote. They are not assigned according to merit. They come because life unfolds under heaven in ways we don't manage.

Caregivers often live in a season that feels prolonged and unbalanced, like a harsh winter that won't end. The language of seasons can sound comforting until you realize that some seasons stretch far longer than expected. This verse doesn't promise that the season will end soon. It names something quieter and more difficult. This season counts. It is real time. It isn't a pause before life resumes. It is part of life itself.

Ecclesiastes doesn't ask us to romanticize our season. It asks us to live faithfully within it. Patience, in this wisdom tradition, isn't passively waiting for a better chapter. It is learning how to inhabit the chapter you are in without losing yourself. Perseverance becomes the art of staying human, staying honest, and staying present in a time you didn't choose.

For caregivers, this can be a hard word and a freeing one. You don't have to rush this season to justify it. You don't have to pretend it feels balanced or fair. God meets you in real time, not ideal time. And even here, even in a season that feels too long, your faithfulness matters.

Prayer

God, this season isn't one I would have chosen, and some days it feels heavier than I can name. Help me live faithfully in the time I am given, without rushing ahead or giving up. Meet me here, in this season, and teach me how to endure with honesty and grace. Amen.

Journaling Prompt

What has this current season of caregiving required of you, and how might you practice faithfulness without wishing the time away?

When Night Lingers

God's anger lasts only a moment, but his favor lasts a lifetime.

Weeping may stay all night, but joy comes in the morning.

Psalm 30:5

Psalm 30 is a psalm of thanksgiving, but it isn't a quick or easy one. David writes after being brought close to death and then restored. Whatever the exact circumstances, the psalm makes clear that this wasn't a near miss brushed off lightly. David had cried out. He had feared going "down to the pit." He had wrestled with his own misplaced confidence and with the terrifying possibility that his life, and his voice of praise, might be cut short.

That context matters when we read the familiar line about weeping and joy. David isn't offering a slogan meant to rush grief along. He is reflecting on survival. The psalm moves slowly, beginning with gratitude for deliverance, passing through confession and desperate prayer, and only then arriving at praise. Joy comes in the morning, but only after a long night that David doesn't minimize or forget.

Caregivers know these nights. Some are literal, marked by alarms, pain, or worry that refuses to let sleep come. Others are emotional, seasons where fear and sorrow stretch on far longer than expected. Psalm 30 doesn't promise that the night will be short. It simply insists that the night isn't the final word.

It also helps to notice what joy means here. David's joy isn't the erasure of what happened. It is the gift of restoration, the return of breath, the ability to stand again and give thanks. For caregivers, joy may look less like celebration and more like relief. A moment of steadiness after crisis. A breath taken without fear. A reminder that God has not abandoned you in the darkest hours.

Psalm 30 gives us permission to hold both truths together. Weeping is real, and it may linger. Joy is real too, and it arrives not because suffering was imaginary, but because God is merciful. Hope, in this psalm, isn't denial. It is the quiet confidence that even after the longest night, God still has mornings to give.

Prayer

God, you know how long some nights can feel and how deeply sorrow can settle in. Thank you for staying near when we weep and for bringing light when the darkness lifts. Help me trust that this night isn't the end of the story, and that your mercy still has mornings ahead. Amen.

Journaling Prompt

What kind of "night" have you been living in recently, and where have you glimpsed even a small sign that God's mercy is still at work?

When the Path Feels Wrong

Trust in the Lord with all your heart;
don't rely on your own intelligence.
Know him in all your paths,
and he will keep your ways straight.

Proverbs 3:5–6

This is one of those verses that sounds beautiful until life turns sharply in a direction you would never have chosen.

"Trust in the Lord with all your heart."
"All your paths."
"He will keep your ways straight."

And then the question rises, sometimes quietly, sometimes in anger:

If he directs paths, why did he direct my loved one down this path? Why did he direct me down this one?

Caregiving has a way of exposing that tension. A diagnosis you didn't ask for. A decline you prayed wouldn't come. A season that feels more like exile than guidance. It can feel less like a straight path and more like a maze you never meant to enter.

Part of our confusion comes from how we imagine direction. We tend to think that if God directs our steps, the road should be smooth, understandable, even efficient.

7

But Proverbs doesn't promise a painless route. It promises guidance within it.

"He will keep your ways straight" doesn't mean he eliminates every detour. It means he makes your path purposeful, even when it's hard. Straight in Scripture often means aligned, not easy. Oriented, not obstacle-free.

Trusting with "all your heart" also means admitting that your understanding is limited. That isn't a rebuke. It is a relief. Caregiving decisions are complicated. Medical updates shift. Outcomes remain uncertain. You don't see the whole picture. You never have.

But trusting doesn't require you to approve of the path. It doesn't demand that you call suffering good. It means placing your weight on God's character when you cannot make sense of God's direction.

Sometimes God's direction isn't about steering you away from hardship, but about steering you through it without losing yourself. Through this path, patience deepens. Compassion stretches. Dependence grows more honest. None of those require the path to be pleasant. They require it to be real.

You may never know why you wound up taking this road. But you can know this: God isn't surprised by it. He isn't scrambling to adjust. He is present in the confusion, not waiting at the end of it.

Trust, in this verse, is less about certainty and more about orientation. It is waking up and saying, "I don't understand this road, but I will walk it with you." It is acknowledging him in hospital corridors, in kitchen cleanups, in paperwork and fatigue and quiet resentment, and trusting that even here, your steps are not random.

Caregiver, your path may feel crooked. It may feel unfair. It may feel unbearably long. But it isn't unnoticed. The God who sees the whole road is still walking it with you, guiding not always by explanation, but by presence.

Prayer

God, I struggle to understand why this is the road we are on. Some days I resent it. Some days I fear it. Teach me to trust you not because I understand, but because you are faithful. Guide my steps when I feel lost, and keep my heart aligned with you even when the path feels confusing. Amen.

Journaling Prompt

What part of your caregiving path feels most confusing or unfair right now? What might it look like to trust God's presence there, even if you cannot trust the explanation?

Not Forgotten in Exile

But those who hope in the Lord will renew their strength;
they will fly up on wings like eagles;
they will run and not be tired;
they will walk and not be weary.

Isaiah 40:31

For more than two decades, we cared for our daughter at home. With the support of a nursing agency for much of that time, we managed the relentless rhythms of ventilator-dependent care. Recently (as I write this), we made the difficult decision to move her into a specialized nursing home for patients who rely on ventilators. The change has brought both relief and grief.

During those years, I returned to Isaiah 40:31 again and again. I clung to the promise of soaring like an eagle. Some days, though, it felt like the eagle had long since flown away.

Eventually I realized I had been reading the verse by itself, missing the larger story.

Isaiah 40 was spoken to people who had lived in exile for decades. Jerusalem was gone. Their lives had been uprooted. Many believed God had abandoned them. Into that despair came the prophet's voice: "Comfort, comfort my people, says your God."

God had not forgotten them. Exile was not the end of their story. A new journey home was coming.

That context changes how I hear verse 31.

The promise isn't that God's people will escape hardship. The exiles still had a long road ahead. The promise is that God would sustain them through it.

And notice the movement in the verse.

First, soaring like eagles.
Then running without collapse.
Finally, walking without giving up.

The last line matters. Most of life isn't soaring. Much of caregiving isn't even running. It is walking. Slow, steady, faithful walking.

Walking down a long hospital corridor.
Walking into another appointment.
Walking through another day of decisions and routines.

Isaiah's promise isn't that caregivers will always feel strong. It is that God renews strength along the way. When we think we cannot take another step, God provides what is needed for the next one.

Sometimes renewal looks dramatic. Often it is quiet: enough patience for one more conversation, enough clarity for one more decision, enough endurance for one more day.

Caregiver, you may not feel like an eagle right now. That doesn't mean the promise has failed. The God who carried Israel through exile is still renewing strength today.

And sometimes His greatest gift is simply this: the strength to keep walking.

Prayer

Father, when I feel worn down and unsure how to keep going, renew my strength. Help me trust that you are sustaining me even when progress feels slow. Give me the endurance to keep walking in faith today. Amen.

Journaling Prompt

Where do you most feel the need for renewed strength right now? What might "keeping walking" look like for you in this season?

Never Alone in the Battle

I've commanded you to be brave and strong, haven't I? Don't be alarmed or terrified, because the Lord your God is with you wherever you go.

Joshua 1:9

Caregiving can feel like being dropped into unfamiliar territory without a map. That's where Joshua stood. Moses was gone. Leadership rested on his shoulders. The future was uncertain. And into that moment, God spoke: Be strong and courageous.

The strength Joshua was commanded to show wasn't self-generated. It rested on one promise: God would be with him.

Caregivers often hear encouragement that sounds like a pep talk. "Stay strong." "Keep going." "You've got this." Even when offered with love, those words can sting. Some days you don't "got this" at all.

Joshua 1:9 reminds us that courage isn't rooted in self-sufficiency. It grows from presence. "The Lord your God is with you wherever you go." Into appointments. Into hospital corridors. Into long nights when sleep won't come.

Tonight, as I write this, our daughter is in a critical care unit. At twenty-two, she's been hospitalized more times than we can count—thirty-five, maybe forty. This is only her second stay in a "big people's hospital." She's been sicker before, but it's sobering to hear doctors ask whether we would want extraordinary measures if her heart stops.

Moments like that surface fear quickly.

And yet, even here, in the hum of machines and the uncertainty of tomorrow, God's presence isn't theoretical. His promise isn't to erase fear. It's to meet us inside it. That's where courage begins—not in denial, but in companionship.

You may not feel strong. You may feel exhausted, frightened, stretched thin. But courage, in Scripture, is less about emotional steadiness and more about refusing to walk alone. The God who spoke to Joshua still goes with his people wherever they go.

Prayer

Father, you know how quickly fear rises when the stakes feel too high. Thank you for going with me into every room and every hard conversation. Help me lean on your presence when I don't have strength of my own. Amen.

Journaling Prompt

What fear feels most immediate right now? How might remembering God's nearness change the way you carry it?

The Lord Is Close

The Lord is close to the brokenhearted,
and he saves those whose spirits are crushed.

Psalm 34:18

Grief is often treated as a moment. Something happens, we mourn, and eventually we're expected to move on. But many caregivers discover that grief isn't confined to a single event. It accumulates.

We have obvious losses: health, independence, a future that looks nothing like what you once imagined. And there are quieter losses that arrive without ceremony. Control. Certainty. Opportunities declined. Friendships that slowly thin. Milestones that never come. Over time, the weight gathers.

Psalm 34 doesn't tell the brokenhearted to be strong. It doesn't rush to explain suffering or assign meaning to it. It says something simpler: the Lord is close.

That word matters.

God doesn't remain at a distance, waiting for grief to resolve itself. He doesn't require you to sort out your emotions before approaching him. Nearness is his first movement toward a crushed spirit.

For caregivers, that can be a quiet relief. You don't have to justify your sorrow by pointing to one defining tragedy.

You don't have to prove that your exhaustion qualifies as grief. God isn't weighing whether your losses are significant enough. He is already near.

Closeness doesn't erase pain. But it does mean you aren't carrying it alone. God draws near not after grief has settled, but while it is still unfolding. In ongoing loss, in unfinished sorrow, in hearts that feel more fractured than healed, his presence remains steady.

If you feel brokenhearted today, you aren't failing. You aren't weak. You are exactly where this psalm speaks—within reach of a God who moves toward crushed spirits rather than away from them.

Prayer

God, you see the grief I carry, both the losses I can name and the ones that have quietly shaped me. When my heart feels worn down and my spirit feels fragile, draw near. Help me trust that I don't grieve alone. Amen.

Journaling Prompt

What losses, large or small, have accumulated in your caregiving journey? Where might you need to notice God's nearness rather than look for quick healing?

Always With You

Look, I myself will be with you every day until the end of this present age.

Matthew 28:20

Caregiving can intensify a particular kind of loneliness. Even when others love you well, there are moments no one else can enter. Three in the morning. A dark room. The steady rhythm of machines. The sense that this stretch of night might never end.

Jesus speaks these words at the close of Matthew's Gospel to disciples he is sending into uncertainty. He doesn't promise them clarity, safety, or ease. He promises presence. "I myself will be with you." Not occasionally. Not only in sacred spaces. Not only when faith feels strong. Every day.

It's worth remembering that Jesus understood what it was to feel alone. In Gethsemane, his closest friends could not stay awake with him. On the cross, he cried out words of abandonment drawn from the psalms. Whether one frames that cry theologically or psychologically, the fact remains: he entered the experience of isolation. He knows what that edge feels like.

Perhaps that is why this promise matters so much. He doesn't offer what he himself refused to enter. He assures his followers that they won't face their calling without companionship.

Caregiving days often blur together, love and labor woven into one long stretch without clear milestones. Through the ache, the paperwork, the quiet prayers you barely have energy to form, his presence doesn't withdraw. It doesn't fade when patience thins or when exhaustion settles deep in your bones.

You may not *feel* accompanied. But presence isn't measured by emotion. The promise stands whether the room feels full of faith or hollow with fatigue.

You are not serving alone.

The One who has known the weight of isolation walks with you through hospital corridors, kitchen cleanups, and silent hours when no one else is awake. And he doesn't leave.

Prayer

Lord Jesus, you know what it is to feel alone. When loneliness presses in and the night feels long, remind me that you are still here. Stay with me in the quiet hours, and help me trust your presence even when I cannot feel it. Amen.

Journaling Prompt

Where have you felt most alone in your caregiving journey? How does it change your perspective to remember that Jesus understands that feeling?

Nothing Can Separate Us

I'm convinced that nothing can separate us from God's love in Christ Jesus our Lord: not death or life, not angels or rulers, not present things or future things, not powers or height or depth, or any other thing that is created.

Romans 8:38–39

When we hear Paul say that neither death nor life can separate us from God's love, death makes sense. Death feels like the ultimate separation. Of course he would name that.

But life?

How could life separate us?

Caregiving helps us understand. It isn't always a single catastrophic moment that tests faith. Sometimes it's the long stretch of ordinary days. The repetition. The appointments. The fatigue that settles into your bones. The slow reshaping of your world. The steady weight of responsibility that doesn't lift.

That is life.

And some days, that life can feel like distance.

Paul doesn't ignore that possibility. He names life as something that might seem powerful enough to wedge itself between us and the love of God. Then he says it cannot.

He goes further. Not "anything that is created." Illness is created. Time is created. Hospital rooms are created. The

19

body itself, fragile and magnificent, is created. Even death belongs to the created order.

None of it outranks the love of God.

That doesn't mean caregiving won't exhaust you. It doesn't mean grief won't accumulate or that long seasons won't wear you thin. It means that the daily grind, as relentless as it can feel, doesn't loosen God's grip.

You may feel separated from your old routines. From friends. From the future you once imagined. But you are not separated from him.

Paul's confidence isn't loud. It's settled. Nothing in all creation has the authority to untether you from Christ's love. Not crisis. Not chronic strain. Not even the slow erosion of strength that comes from simply living through hard days.

You may feel worn down. You may feel diminished. But you are not unloved. And you are not beyond the reach of the love that holds you fast.

Prayer

God of unbreakable love, some days it's not death that frightens me but the long stretch of living through this season. When the ordinary weight feels heavy, remind me that nothing in all creation can separate me from you. Hold me steady in the daily grind, and keep me anchored in your love. Amen.

Journaling Prompt

Where has the ordinary strain of caregiving felt most separating to you? How does it change your perspective to remember that even "life" itself cannot separate you from God's love?

You may feel worn down.
You may feel diminished.
But you are not unloved.
And you are not beyond the
reach of the love that
holds you fast.

Never Forsaken

The Lord is the one who will go before you; he will be with you. He won't leave you or abandon you. So don't be afraid or terrified.

Deuteronomy 31:8

Joshua did not volunteer for this moment. Moses died. Leadership shifted. The responsibility landed squarely on his shoulders.

He had been faithful for years. One of the two spies who trusted God when others panicked. One of the few who survived forty years of wilderness wandering. He did not seek the role, but he had been shaped for it.

Caregiving often arrives the same way. You may not have applied for this calling. You may not have imagined yourself here. Yet somehow the weight rests with you. Not because you are fearless, but because you are steady. Not because you wanted it, but because you have endured before.

In that moment of transfer, Moses tells Joshua something distinct: the Lord will go before you.

Not only with you. Before you.

Before the battle. Before the uncertainty. Before the fear has time to grow roots.

That promise matters for caregivers. Much of the anxiety you carry is about what's next. The next appointment. The next decline. The next decision you hope you won't have to make. Anticipation can be heavier than the present moment.

But God is already there.

He is already present in tomorrow's conversation. Already in the hospital room you haven't entered yet. Already in the outcome you cannot predict. You are not the first one stepping into what frightens you.

And just as Joshua had been formed through years in the wilderness, you have been shaped by what you have already survived. Faithfulness rarely feels heroic. It feels like showing up again. And again. And again.

You may not have chosen this responsibility. But it did not surprise God. The One who goes before you also remains with you. The future you fear isn't empty. It is already inhabited by his presence.

Prayer

Lord, I did not ask for this responsibility, and some days it feels larger than I am. When I fear what lies ahead, remind me that you are already there. Give me courage not because I feel strong, but because you go before me. Amen.

Journaling Prompt

What future moment feels most daunting right now? How does it shift your perspective to remember that God is already present there?

Held When You Feel Unsteady

Don't fear, because I am with you;
don't be afraid, for I am your God.
I will strengthen you;
I will surely help you;
I will hold you with my righteous strong hand.

Isaiah 41:10

Isaiah speaks these words to people in exile—displaced, diminished, and uncertain of their future. They were not fragile because they lacked faith. They were fragile because their world had been overturned.

That context matters.

The promise isn't abstract. It is intensely physical. "I will hold you with my righteous strong hand."

Caregiving exposes how quickly we can lose our footing. Some days you feel steady. Other days, one unexpected phone call is enough to unravel you. Plans shift. Symptoms worsen. What felt manageable in the morning feels impossible by night.

Isaiah doesn't pretend that fear won't surface. "Don't fear" isn't denial. It is invitation. The command rests on a promise: you will be held.

The image here isn't of God offering advice from a distance. It is of a grip. The righteous hand isn't merely powerful; it is faithful. It acts in line with who God is. Steady. Consistent. Unwavering.

We often wish the promise said, "I will remove what threatens you." Instead, it says, "I will strengthen you. I will help you. I will hold you."

Strength, in this passage, is supplied. Not summoned. You are not commanded to manufacture resilience. You are promised reinforcement.

There are moments in caregiving when you realize you have passed your own limits. You are tired beyond what feels sustainable. Emotionally thin. Physically worn. Spiritually depleted. Isaiah doesn't deny that. It assumes it.

Being upheld means the weight isn't entirely yours. Even when responsibility rests heavily in your hands, there is a stronger hand beneath them.

You may feel unsteady today. But you are not unsupported. The God who sustained exiles through long uncertainty still strengthens and upholds. Not always by removing the strain, but by refusing to let you collapse without support.

Prayer

God, some days I feel like my footing is slipping. Fear rises quickly, and my strength runs thin. Thank you for promising not just presence, but support. Hold me steady when I cannot steady myself. Amen.

Journaling Prompt

Where do you feel closest to your limits right now? What might it mean to imagine God's strong hand beneath yours in that place?

When Weakness Becomes Power

I was given a thorn in my body because of the outstanding revelations I've received so that I wouldn't be conceited. It's a messenger from Satan sent to torment me so that I wouldn't be conceited.

I pleaded with the Lord three times for it to leave me alone. He said to me, "My grace is enough for you, because power is made perfect in weakness." So I'll gladly spend my time bragging about my weaknesses so that Christ's power can rest on me. Therefore, I'm all right with weaknesses, insults, disasters, harassments, and stressful situations for the sake of Christ, because when I'm weak, then I'm strong.

2 Corinthians 12:7–10

We don't know what Paul's thorn was. That silence may be a gift. It allows every generation to recognize its own version of something that won't leave.

What we do know is that Paul asked for relief. Repeatedly. He didn't suffer in silence. He didn't pretend the thorn felt pleasant. He wanted it *gone*.

Many caregivers understand that prayer. We've pleaded for healing. For reversal. For the burden to lift. Not because we don't love the one in our care, but because the weight is relentless. And sometimes the prayer becomes complicated. We want relief, yet we recoil from what relief might mean.

That tension is real.

Paul doesn't receive removal. He receives grace.

"My grace is enough for you." Not, "The thorn will disappear." Not, "You will grow to enjoy this." Grace, instead, becomes the sustaining presence within what remains.

I remember caring for our daughter through two weeks of blizzard conditions without power. No heat. No light. No comfort. Just the steady exhaustion of keeping her safe in circumstances we couldn't control. We did not rise to heroism. We survived. And in the surviving, something steadied us that was not purely our own resolve.

"When I'm weak, then I'm strong" doesn't mean weakness becomes pleasant. It means weakness becomes the place where Christ's power settles. Strength, here, isn't independence. It is dependence that doesn't collapse.

You may not come to love the thorn. You may not even come to accept it easily. But grace can meet you there. Not as a substitute for the burden, but as support within it.

Prayer

Lord, I have asked for relief more than once. You know how weary I become, how love and frustration can live side by side in me. If the thorn remains, let your grace be enough for today. Let your strength rest on me where I am weakest. Amen.

Journaling Prompt

What "thorn" feels most persistent in your caregiving right now? Where might you need to ask not only for removal, but for sustaining grace?

The Slower Yoke

Come to me, all you who are struggling hard and carrying heavy loads, and I will give you rest. Put on my yoke, and learn from me. I'm gentle and humble. And you will find rest for yourselves.

Matthew 11:28–29

We often hear this as a promise of removal. Come to Jesus, and the weight disappears.

But that isn't what he says.

He invites the weary to come—and then to take on a yoke. Not escape, but apprenticeship. Not the absence of responsibility, but shared responsibility.

A yoke isn't decorative. It is working equipment. It links two animals so they pull together. Jesus doesn't promise that caregivers will have no load. He promises they won't carry it alone.

For many caregivers, life feels like one prolonged emergency. Even when things are stable, the body remains braced. Waiting. Listening. Preparing for the next shift. Rest feels like collapse between crises.

But the rest Jesus offers is different. It isn't merely recovery. It is reorientation.

"Learn from me," he says.

Learn how to carry weight without being crushed by it. Learn how to move without frantic urgency. Learn how to remain gentle when the pressure rises. Learn how to stay anchored when circumstances refuse to cooperate.

Jesus describes himself as gentle and humble. That matters. He isn't harsh with the weary. He doesn't shame the exhausted. His strength isn't frantic or brittle. It is steady.

When you are yoked to someone stronger, the burden distributes. The stronger one bears more of the strain. You still walk. You still labor. But the load no longer rests entirely on your shoulders.

Caregiving may not grow lighter. But it can grow shared.

Rest, then, isn't the absence of responsibility. It is the relief of knowing that the weight isn't yours alone to sustain.

Prayer

Lord Jesus, I am tired of carrying this weight as if it depends entirely on me. Teach me how to walk with you, not apart from you. Share the burden I am holding, and form in me your gentle strength. Amen.

Journaling Prompt

Where do you feel as if the entire burden rests on you? What might it look like to imagine Jesus carrying the heavier side of that load?

The Slow Work of Perseverance

My brothers and sisters, think of the various tests you encounter as occasions for joy. After all, you know that the testing of your faith produces endurance. And let endurance do what it's supposed to do so that you may be mature and complete, lacking in nothing.

James 1:2–4

James can sound abrupt if we read him too quickly. "Consider it joy" doesn't feel natural when life is already heavy. Caregiving trials are not hypothetical. They have names. Diagnoses. Deadlines. Responsibilities that don't loosen their grip.

But James doesn't us to *enjoy* suffering. He asks us to see it differently.

He points to a slow process. Testing produces endurance. Not instantly. Not dramatically. Over time.

Endurance is the quiet ability to keep going. It is built in repetition—getting up again, making the call, giving the medication, staying present when you would rather withdraw. It rarely feels impressive. It just feels necessary.

What stands out is James' instruction to let endurance "do its work." That implies we often resist it. We want resolution. We want the trial to end so life can return to something recognizable. But caregiving usually doesn't offer clean endings. Sometimes the work is simply staying.

Endurance, then, becomes formative, not by hardening you, but by deepening you. It stretches your capacity. It enlarges your patience. It exposes your limits and teaches you how to live within them. None of that feels triumphant in the moment.

"Mature and complete" doesn't mean flawless or untroubled. It means integrated. Whole. Not fragmented by pressure. Not defined solely by what you are enduring.

James doesn't promise that the trial itself is good. He suggests that perseverance within it isn't wasted. Even in a season you would never have chosen, something steady is being built, not sainthood, but endurance.

Prayer

God, I don't naturally feel joy in this struggle. Some days I simply feel tired. If endurance is being formed in me, help it grow without hardening my heart. Give me grace to keep showing up, and shape me into someone whole. Amen.

Journaling Prompt

Where is endurance being asked of you right now? How might you allow it to deepen you without letting it make you hard?

When Waiting Is the Work

Be still before the Lord, and wait patiently for him. Don't get upset when someone gets ahead—someone who invents evil schemes.

Psalm 37:7

The psalmist didn't write Psalm 37 from the edge of disaster. It is wisdom poetry, shaped to be read slowly and returned to. Rather than a single crisis, it addresses the steady shaping of the heart over time.

One word threads through the psalm again and again: fret.

Fret when others prosper. Fret when justice feels delayed. Fret when doing the right thing doesn't seem to change anything.

"Be still before the Lord," the psalmist says. "Wait patiently."

This isn't passivity. It is restraint of the soul.

Caregivers know this tension. Outwardly, you are anything but still. You are scheduling appointments, managing medications, staying alert. But inwardly, agitation can hum constantly beneath the surface: Why is this taking so long? Why isn't anything improving? How much longer can this go on?

Psalm 37 doesn't deny frustration. It names what fretting does over time. It erodes trust. It distorts perspective. It quietly corrodes joy.

The psalm also warns about comparison. Watching others "get ahead" can stir resentment. For caregivers, that comparison may not center on wealth or status, but on freedom. Other families travel. Other lives look lighter. Other people seem to move forward while you remain in place.

Comparison intensifies restlessness.

Waiting patiently, in this psalm, isn't resignation. It is allegiance. It is choosing not to let agitation rule your inner life. It is anchoring yourself to God's timing instead of being driven by the apparent ease of others.

Psalm 37 doesn't promise speed. It promises steadiness.

And in long caregiving seasons, steadiness is no small gift.

Prayer

God, fretting comes more easily than stillness. I feel the quiet agitation in my heart when progress is slow and others seem unburdened. Teach me how to wait without growing bitter. Anchor me in your steadiness when impatience starts to take over. Amen.

Journaling Prompt

Where does comparison or impatience most often stir restlessness in you? What would it look like to practice inner stillness in that specific place?

Waiting for What Will Grow

Let's not get tired of doing good, because in time we'll have a harvest if we don't give up.

Galatians 6:9

I grew up in West Tennessee, where life followed the rhythm of the fields. My family weren't farmers, but nearly everyone around us was. In those days the fields were cotton. Now they're mostly soybeans. Either way, planting required faith.

Perfectly good seed went into the ground with no guarantee of what the season would bring. Farmers worked daily—planting, fertilizing, repairing equipment, watching the weather. Weeks passed with little visible evidence that anything was happening. Growth took place out of sight.

Paul draws on that same image when he writes about harvest. We plant. We water. God gives the growth. The outcome doesn't rest entirely in our hands.

Caregiving often feels like tending a field that doesn't respond quickly. You show up. You give medication. You make calls. You advocate. You pray. Some days it seems as if nothing changes. The condition remains. The struggle continues. The field looks the same.

Galatians doesn't promise immediate results. It speaks to weariness. "Don't get tired of doing good." That implies fatigue is normal. Discouragement is expected.

The harvest Paul mentions may not look like cure or dramatic improvement. Sometimes the harvest is quieter: a moment of dignity preserved, a relationship deepened, a heart softened, a resilience you didn't know you possessed. Sometimes the harvest is simply faithfulness that endured.

You cannot force growth. You can only keep tending.

And God is at work beneath the surface, in ways you may never fully see.

Prayer

Father, I grow tired when I don't see results. Help me keep doing good without demanding immediate proof that it matters. Remind me that you are working in ways I cannot measure, and give me strength not to give up. Amen.

Journaling Prompt

Where do you feel most tempted to give up right now? What might it look like to trust that something unseen is still taking root?

The Long Race, Faithfully Run

So then, with endurance, let's run the race that is laid out in front of us, since we have such a great cloud of witnesses surrounding us. Let's throw off any extra baggage, get rid of the sin that trips us up, and fix our eyes on Jesus, faith's pioneer and perfecter. He endured the cross, ignoring the shame, for the sake of the joy that was laid out before him, and sat down at the right side of God's throne.

Hebrews 12:1–2

Hebrews doesn't describe a sprint. It describes a long race—one already laid out.

That detail matters. The course is assigned, not selected. Much of our exhaustion comes from wishing we were running a different one.

Caregiving often feels exactly like that. You look at the lane you're in and think, I wouldn't have chosen this. Hebrews doesn't ask you to like the race. It asks you to run the one before you—with endurance.

The writer also speaks of a "great cloud of witnesses." Not spectators waiting to criticize your pace, but witnesses who have endured before you. Their presence reminds us that long faithfulness is possible. Others have walked hard roads and finished them without abandoning trust.

There is honesty here about weight. Some burdens are unavoidable. You cannot simply shrug off responsibility. But not everything you carry is required. Guilt that you are not doing enough. Comparison with families who seem freer. The pressure to be endlessly patient. Those can become extra baggage.

Endurance isn't carrying everything. It is carrying what is yours, and releasing what isn't.

Then comes the focus: "Fix your eyes on Jesus."

He endured the cross—and the shame. That word matters. Shame isolates. It whispers that suffering is somehow your failure. Caregivers know that voice. You replay decisions. You wonder if you missed something. You feel exposed in moments you never asked for.

Jesus endured shame without letting it define him. He did not deny the suffering. He endured it with purpose, holding onto a joy not yet visible.

Fixing your eyes on him doesn't shorten the race. It clarifies it. It reminds you that endurance isn't about proving strength. It is about staying faithful to the course you've been given.

This race may be long. It may not look like anyone else's. But it isn't random. And you are not the first to run something hard.

Prayer

Jesus, some days I resent the course in front of me. I carry more than I need to, and I grow tired of the distance still ahead. Help me release what isn't mine to bear. Teach me to fix my eyes on you and keep running with steady faith. Amen.

Journaling Prompt

What feels like "extra baggage" in your caregiving right now? How might focusing on Jesus change the way you carry what remains?

Strength for the Weary

"Don't be sad, because the joy from the Lord is your strength."

Nehemiah 8:10

Nehemiah 8 isn't a lighthearted celebration. The people have returned from exile. The walls are rebuilt, but their spiritual life has been in ruins. When the Law is read aloud, they weep. They hear how far they have drifted. They feel the weight of what was lost.

Their tears are not rebuked as inappropriate. They are simply not allowed to be the final word.

"Don't be sad," Nehemiah says. "The joy from the Lord is your strength."

This isn't emotional denial. It is theological recalibration.

The people stand in a restored city. They are hearing God's Word again. The very fact that they are gathered is evidence of mercy. Their return isn't the result of their perfection, but of God's covenant faithfulness.

Caregiving can carry a similar mixture of grief and shame. There are losses you cannot undo. Decisions you replay. Days when you feel you have fallen short. Exhaustion can blur into self-criticism.

Into that moment comes this phrase: the joy of the Lord.

Not your joy about the situation. Not forced cheerfulness. Not gratitude manufactured on demand. The joy of the Lord refers to God's settled commitment to his people. His covenant delight. His refusal to abandon what he has chosen to love.

That joy becomes strength.

Strength here doesn't mean energy or optimism. It means stability. It means you are not defined by your worst day. It means the story isn't measured solely by what has gone wrong.

The people in Nehemiah's day were told to eat, drink, and share food with those who had nothing prepared. Joy moved them outward. It steadied them enough to reenter life together.

You may not feel joyful today. But your strength doesn't depend on how bright your mood is. It rests in a God who has not withdrawn his commitment from you.

Even in weariness. Even in imperfection.

Prayer

Father, I often measure myself by what feels lacking. When sorrow and self-doubt weigh on me, remind me that your commitment to me has not shifted. Let your steady joy become the strength that keeps me grounded today. Amen.

Journaling Prompt

Where do sorrow or self-criticism most drain your strength right now? How might remembering God's steady commitment reshape the way you see yourself in this season?

Peace That Holds When You Can't

Don't be anxious about anything; rather, bring up all of your requests to God in your prayers and petitions, along with giving thanks. Then the peace of God that exceeds all understanding will keep your hearts and minds safe in Christ Jesus.

Philippians 4:6–7

Caregivers learn quickly that worry comes easily, rest doesn't. When someone you love is hurting, prayer can become a running list of urgent requests. That isn't wrong. Love naturally speaks in pleas.

Paul doesn't rebuke the requests. He expands them.

Bring everything, he says—petitions and thanksgiving together.

Thanksgiving can feel out of place when anxiety is loud. Yet gratitude isn't denial. It is recognition. Strength you did not expect. A friend who checks in. A moment of steadiness in the middle of chaos. A small mercy that arrived unannounced. Naming these doesn't erase fear, but it widens the frame.

Then Paul makes a remarkable promise. The peace of God will guard your hearts and minds.

The word is protective. Military. Peace stands watch.

Caregiving often feels like an open door to constant intrusion. What if the test results worsen? What if I missed something? What happens next month? Anxiety doesn't knock politely. It storms in.

God's peace doesn't promise the absence of threat. It promises protection of the inner life. It keeps watch over your thoughts. It steadies your heart when scenarios multiply.

This peace "exceeds understanding." It isn't logical calm based on resolved circumstances. It is steadiness that doesn't fully make sense given what remains uncertain.

You may still face difficult news. You may still feel concern. But you don't have to let anxiety govern the space inside you.

Prayer isn't a technique for controlling outcomes. It is the act of placing your whole bundle of fear and gratitude into God's hands—and allowing his peace to take up its post at the door of your heart.

Prayer

Father, anxiety comes quickly and easily. Teach me to bring all of it to you—my fears and my gratitude together. Let your peace stand guard over my thoughts when they begin to spiral. Keep my heart steady in Christ. Amen.

Journaling Prompt

Where does anxiety most often invade your thoughts? What might it look like to imagine God's peace standing watch there?

God's Comfort in a Crowded Head

When my anxieties multiplied, your consolations brought me joy.

Psalm 94:19

Psalm 94 isn't written from a quiet place. It rises from pressure—oppression, injustice, the sense that wrong is going unanswered. In that setting, the psalmist names something deeply familiar: anxiety multiplies.

It rarely travels alone.

One concern triggers another. A medical update raises three new questions. A long night awakens older fears. Thoughts stack on top of each other until it feels impossible to sort them out.

The psalm doesn't say the anxieties vanished. It says God's consolations met them.

That distinction matters.

Consolation isn't explanation. It doesn't answer every "why." It doesn't restore control. It steadies rather than solves. It enters while the mind is still racing.

For caregivers, this feels true. Relief doesn't always come in the form of changed circumstances. Sometimes it comes as a moment of unexpected calm. A Scripture that settles. A friend's voice at the right time. A sense, however brief, that you are not unraveling as much as you feared.

43

Joy, in this verse, isn't brightness. It is relief. It is the exhale that follows being understood. It is the quiet shift from isolation to awareness: I am not alone inside this storm of thoughts.

Anxiety may still multiply. But consolation multiplies too.

God's comfort doesn't wait for your mind to quiet down. It meets you in the noise and holds its ground there.

Prayer

Father, my worries stack faster than I can sort them. Thank you that your comfort doesn't require perfect calm. Meet me in the noise. Let your consolations steady me when anxiety begins to multiply. Amen.

Journaling Prompt

When your thoughts begin to stack and spiral, what has helped you recognize God's consolation in the middle of it?

Where the Mind Rests

You will keep in perfect peace those whose minds are stayed on you, because they trust in you.

Isaiah 26:3

Isaiah speaks these words in the middle of instability. Nations rise and fall. Security feels fragile. The promise of "perfect peace" isn't offered in calm conditions, but in uncertainty.

The Hebrew repeats the word: shalom shalom. Not just quiet feelings, but settled wholeness. Stability that holds.

The phrase "stayed on you" isn't casual. It suggests leaning. Bracing. Fixing one's weight somewhere solid. It doesn't imply effortless concentration. It implies allegiance.

Caregiving trains the mind to scan for threat. What changed? What did I miss? What happens next? Attention becomes hyper-alert by necessity. That vigilance serves a purpose. But it can also exhaust the soul.

Isaiah doesn't promise that anxious thoughts will vanish. He describes what happens when the mind has somewhere trustworthy to land.

Trust, here, isn't optimism. It is placement. It is deciding, again and again, where your inner weight rests. Not on outcomes. Not on your ability to foresee every risk. Not

45

on rehearsing worst-case scenarios. But on the character of God.

"Perfect peace" doesn't mean the environment is calm. It means the center holds.

For caregivers, that peace may not feel dramatic. It may look like refusing to let fear be the final authority in your thoughts. It may mean acknowledging uncertainty while anchoring yourself to something steadier than the uncertainty.

You cannot prevent every anxious thought. But you can choose where your trust settles.

And over time, that settled trust becomes its own kind of stability.

Prayer

God, my mind is often alert, scanning, bracing for what might go wrong. Help me lean my weight on you instead of carrying it alone. Let your steady character become the place my trust rests. Keep my center from giving way. Amen.

Journaling Prompt

When uncertainty rises, where does your inner weight tend to rest? What would it mean to place that weight more deliberately on God's steadiness?

Throw It Off

Throw all your anxiety onto him, because he cares about you.

1 Peter 5:7

Peter doesn't use gentle language. "Throw" is forceful. Urgent. Deliberate. Anxiety isn't something to cradle or analyze endlessly. It is something to hurl off your shoulders.

Just before this verse, Peter tells his readers to humble themselves under God's mighty hand. That connection matters. Casting anxiety isn't weakness. It is humility.

Caregivers know how easily anxiety disguises itself as responsibility. If I stop worrying, I might miss something. If I relax, something could fall apart. Worry feels like vigilance. It feels like love.

But anxiety can also be a quiet attempt at control. It whispers that if you hold the fear tightly enough, you can manage the outcome.

Peter interrupts that illusion.

Throw it.

Not because your concerns are imaginary. Not because everything will resolve neatly. But because the burden of ultimate control was never assigned to you.

"Because he cares about you."

That phrase isn't sentimental. It is stabilizing. God's care isn't fragile. It doesn't depend on your mental grip. It doesn't increase when you worry harder. His care is already active.

Casting anxiety isn't denial. It is a reallocation of weight. It is admitting that some things exceed your authority. It is trusting that God's care extends not only to the one you are tending, but also to you.

And yes, the throwing may need to happen repeatedly. Anxiety returns. New fears arise. Each time, the invitation remains: you don't have to carry this as if everything depends on you.

You are responsible for faithfulness. Not for control.

Prayer

Father, I cling to worry as if it proves my devotion. Teach me the humility of release. Help me throw onto you what was never mine to control. Remind me that your care is already at work, even when I loosen my grip. Amen.

Journaling Prompt

Where might anxiety be masking a desire for control in your caregiving? What would it mean to entrust that area to God's care rather than gripping it tightly?

When You Don't Walk It Perfectly

The Lord establishes the steps of those who delight in him;
he delights in their way.
If they stumble, they won't be defeated,
because the Lord holds their hand.

Psalm 37:23–24

Caregiving rarely feels like a smooth path. It feels like uneven ground. You make the best decision you can, and new information surfaces. You speak from fatigue and wish you could take the words back. You replay conversations at night, wondering if you missed something.

Psalm 37 meets that reality with clarity.

"The Lord establishes the steps… he delights in their way."

Delight is a strong word. It doesn't mean approval of flawless performance. It means relational pleasure. God isn't merely tolerating your effort. He takes joy in faithful intention, even when execution is imperfect.

Then comes the promise caregivers may need most: "If they stumble, they won't be defeated."

Stumbling is assumed. It isn't rebellion. It is limitation. Weariness. Humanity under strain. Caregivers stumble. You forget something small. You misjudge your capacity. You lose patience. You cannot anticipate every outcome.

The psalm doesn't equate misstep with failure.

Why? "Because the Lord holds their hand."

The image is steadying, not sentimental. A hand held doesn't prevent every wobble. It prevents the fall from becoming final. It keeps movement possible.

God's guidance here isn't rigid control. It is relational support. He establishes your steps, yes—but he also remains close enough to steady you when they falter.

Caregiving can make you harsh with yourself. The stakes feel too high for mistakes. But this psalm offers a gentler truth: you are not one stumble away from disqualification.

You may falter. You may get it wrong sometimes. And still, you are not defeated.

The One who orders your steps is also the One who refuses to let go.

Prayer

God, I know I don't walk this road perfectly. I stumble in decisions, words, and patience. Thank you that my missteps are not the end of the story. Hold my hand when I falter, and steady me so I can keep going. Amen.

Journaling Prompt

Where have you treated a recent misstep as a defeat? How might it change your perspective to imagine God still holding your hand in that moment?

Bound, Not Rushed

He heals the brokenhearted
and binds up their wounds.

Psalm 147:3

We often imagine healing as decisive. A turning point. A clear moment when what was broken is fixed and life resumes its former shape.

Psalm 147 offers something quieter.

God heals the brokenhearted by binding their wounds.

Binding is careful work. It takes time. It requires touch. A bound wound is still a wound. It still aches. It still needs attention. But it is no longer unattended.

Psalm 147 is a song of restoration after exile. The people have returned home, but they are not untouched by what they endured. Restoration doesn't erase what happened. It tends what remains.

That distinction matters in grief.

Some losses don't resolve cleanly. Over years of caregiving—and sometimes long after it ends—sorrow becomes layered. One grief settles before another rises. The heart learns to live with wounds that are managed rather than removed.

This psalm doesn't shame that reality. It doesn't rush toward closure. It portrays a God who works patiently with what is fragile. One who stays near enough to notice where the wound still opens. One who returns to tend it again.

For caregivers, that can be a relief. You are not failing because pain resurfaces. You are not faithless because memory still stings. Healing, here, isn't forgetting. It is faithful care over time.

God binds wounds the way a skilled healer would—attentive, deliberate, unhurried. Not dismissing the injury. Not pretending it no longer hurts.

If your heart still carries tenderness, Psalm 147 doesn't tell you to move on. It tells you that God is at work in the tending itself.

Healing, in this psalm, isn't a finish line. It is an ongoing act of mercy.

Prayer

God, my heart carries wounds that have not disappeared with time. Thank you for tending them with patience instead of pressure. Stay near to what remains fragile in me, and help me trust your steady care, even when the ache lingers. Amen.

Journaling Prompt

What wounds feel tended but not erased in your life right now? How might it reshape your expectations to see healing as ongoing care rather than sudden resolution?

Morning by Morning

The Lord's loyal love hasn't run out; his compassion doesn't fail.
They are renewed every morning.
Great is your faithfulness.

Lamentations 3:22–23

Lamentations isn't light reading. It is poetry written in the aftermath of destruction. Jerusalem lies in ruins. The people are displaced, disoriented, grieving. The book doesn't hurry toward comfort. It lingers in loss.

That context matters.

These words about mercy are not spoken after restoration. They rise from within devastation. The writer has already named despair, bitterness, exhaustion, and the sense of being worn down to nothing. Only then does he say that God's loyal love has not run out.

Hope here isn't optimism. It is survival faith.

"New every morning" doesn't mean the morning feels bright. It means mercy arrives even when circumstances don't improve. The city is still broken. The grief is still present. Yet compassion has not failed.

Caregivers recognize this rhythm. You wake to the same diagnosis, the same responsibilities, the same uncertainties. Nothing dramatic has shifted. And yet there is enough for this day. Not enough to solve everything. Not enough to foresee the future. Enough to rise. Enough to tend. Enough to endure until evening.

That is what faithfulness looks like in Lamentations. Not denial of devastation, but trust that mercy has not been exhausted.

You don't have to minimize your grief to receive God's compassion. You don't have to sound hopeful to be held by faithfulness. Mercy meets you where you wake up, not where you wish you were.

Morning after morning.

Prayer

God, some mornings feel heavy before I even rise. Thank you that your mercy doesn't depend on my energy or outlook. Meet me here, in this ordinary and unfinished day, with compassion that is enough. Amen.

Journaling Prompt

When you think of "mercy for today," what does that look like in your current season? Where have you seen faithfulness show up without fanfare?

Love Beyond Feelings

Love is patient, love is kind, it isn't jealous, it doesn't brag, it isn't arrogant, it isn't rude, it doesn't seek its own advantage, it isn't irritable, it doesn't keep a record of complaints, it isn't happy with injustice, but it is happy with the truth. Love puts up with all things, trusts in all things, hopes for all things, endures all things.

1 Corinthians 13:4–7

This passage is often read at weddings, but Paul wrote it to a fractured church. People were competing, posturing, insisting on their own importance. In that setting, love was not sentiment. It was correction.

Agape love isn't primarily about feeling warmly toward someone. It is about choosing the good of another, again and again.

Caregiving brings that into sharp focus. Affection matters, but the love that carries caregiving is often quieter. It sets alarms for medication. It listens to the same story without rolling its eyes. It cleans up again. It adjusts plans without announcement. It shows up when no one is watching.

My daughter, Hannah, has taught me more about this love than any book. Living within her needs has exposed how often love requires relinquishment—letting go of the day I expected, the schedule I preferred, the control I wanted.

Caregiving resists rigidity. Patience becomes less a virtue you admire and more a necessity you practice.

Paul's description of love can feel overwhelming. "Isn't irritable." "Doesn't keep a record." Anyone who has cared for someone long-term knows how quickly irritation can surface and how easily memory keeps score.

The point isn't perfection. It is direction.

Love endures not because frustration never appears, but because frustration doesn't get the final word. Love returns. It recalibrates. It chooses again.

When Paul speaks of love's endurance, he is describing a durability that reflects God's own posture toward us. Not flawless performance, but steady commitment.

Caregiving gives you daily opportunity to practice that kind of love. Not dramatically. Not romantically. Just faithfully.

Prayer

Father, I don't love perfectly. Irritation rises. Fatigue shortens my patience. Thank you that your love toward me is steady even when mine wavers. Teach me to return to love when I drift, and to choose it again in the small moments that fill my days. Amen.

Journaling Prompt

Where has love required relinquishment in your caregiving recently? When have you had to choose it again after irritation surfaced?

Giving Your Life, One Day at a Time

I have said these things to you so that my joy will be in you and your joy will be complete. This is my commandment: love each other just as I have loved you. No one has greater love than to give up one's life for one's friends.

John 15:11–13

When we hear Jesus speak of laying down one's life, we imagine something dramatic—a split-second act of courage, a headline-worthy sacrifice. Those moments deserve honor.

But for many caregivers, giving up one's life looks different. It isn't a single event. It is accumulation.

It is the steady surrender of time, energy, ambition, convenience. It is saying no to one opportunity so you can say yes to someone who needs you. It is living in a posture of interruption.

I gave my life for my daughter, Hannah, not in one heroic moment, but in years of ordinary decisions. My wife gave hers too, often absorbing what my divided attention left undone. Self-giving love is rarely clean or balanced. It stretches everyone involved.

Caregiving doesn't usually look like glory. It looks like consistency.

Jesus' love followed that same pattern. Before the cross, there were years of walking dusty roads, teaching patiently, touching the untouchable, staying present to need. The cross was the culmination of a life already given.

And yet Jesus connects this self-giving love with joy.

That may sound strange in a life that feels poured thin. But his joy isn't rooted in comfort. It is rooted in alignment with the Father's will. It is the deep coherence of living in harmony with love itself.

Laying down your life in caregiving doesn't mean erasing yourself. It means offering yourself. There is a difference. Erasure breeds resentment. Offering carries purpose.

When your sacrifices flow from love rather than compulsion, something steadier than emotion begins to form. Not constant happiness. Not dramatic fulfillment. But a quiet sense that your life, however constrained, isn't wasted.

Jesus' command isn't heroic spectacle. It is daily faithfulness.

And in that faithfulness, his joy isn't absent.

Prayer

Father, I don't always feel joyful in the giving of myself. Some days it feels costly and unbalanced. Guard me from resentment and from self-erasure. Teach me to offer my life in love, not in bitterness, and let your deeper joy steady me when I feel poured out. Amen.

Journaling Prompt

Where does your caregiving feel like self-offering, and where does it risk becoming self-erasure? How might Christ's pattern of love reshape that difference?

As Unto the Lord

Whatever you do, do it from the heart for the Lord and not for people. You know that you will receive an inheritance as a reward. You serve the Lord Christ.

Colossians 3:23–24

Paul wrote these words to believers living ordinary lives under ordinary pressures. Many of them had little control over their circumstances. Yet Paul reframes their daily work: you are not ultimately working for human approval. You serve the Lord Christ.

That shift of audience matters.

Caregiving often happens out of sight. There are no headlines for cleaning feeding tubes, managing medications, or sitting through long nights of watchfulness. Much of it feels invisible. When gratitude is sparse and recognition rare, motivation can thin.

Paul doesn't say the work will become glamorous. He says it belongs to Christ.

Doing something "for the Lord" doesn't make it instantly meaningful in an emotional sense. It doesn't remove fatigue. It does, however, change the direction of your service. You are not performing for applause or measuring your worth by someone else's response. You are offering your labor to the One who sees without exaggerating or overlooking.

The word "inheritance" reminds us that this life isn't the full accounting. Caregiving can feel like constant output with little visible return. Paul quietly insists that faithfulness isn't lost in the larger story God is telling.

This doesn't mean every moment feels holy. Some moments feel messy, repetitive, even resentful. But even there, your work isn't meaningless.

You serve the Lord Christ.

When you lift, feed, advocate, wait, and repeat, you are not merely completing tasks. You are practicing allegiance. And allegiance doesn't depend on recognition.

Prayer

Father, I often grow tired of work that feels unseen. Reorient my heart when I slip into performing for approval. Help me remember that I serve Christ, not human applause. Let that steady my motives and my spirit. Amen.

Journaling Prompt

Where does caregiving most tempt you to seek recognition or validation? How might remembering who you ultimately serve reshape your perspective?

The One Who Chose to Serve

"For even the Human One didn't come to be served but rather to serve and to give his life to liberate many people."
Mark 10:45, CEB

Jesus speaks these words on the road to Jerusalem, not during a calm devotional moment but in the middle of tension. His disciples are arguing about status. They are imagining rank, proximity, recognition. Jesus doesn't simply correct their behavior. He redefines greatness.

He doesn't say service is admirable. He says it is who he is.

"If anyone had the right to be served…" that is the force of the word even. And yet he defines his life not by what others owe him, but by what he gives. He chooses the downward path. Not because he is powerless, but because this is the shape of his power.

Caregivers know something about that shape.

Much of caregiving is unseen service. It doesn't come with applause. It rarely carries status. Over time, the quiet repetition of giving can begin to feel not only exhausting, but invisible. There are days when it feels like life is being poured out without replenishment.

Jesus doesn't romanticize that cost. He names it. He gives his life.

For most caregivers, "giving your life" isn't one heroic act. It is incremental. It is the slow surrender of control over your schedule, your energy, sometimes even your identity. It is the steady choosing of another person's need over your own preference.

But notice something important. Jesus gives his life to liberate. His service has direction. It has purpose. It isn't self-erasure. It is love aimed toward freedom.

That matters.

Caregiving shaped by Christ isn't about disappearing. It is about aligning your strength with love. It isn't about proving devotion by exhaustion. It is about reflecting the heart of the One who serves.

If caregiving feels like the surrender of the life you imagined, remember this: you are not walking an alien road. Jesus has already walked it. He understands the weight of misunderstood service, the loneliness of unrecognized sacrifice, the cost of loving when it isn't returned in equal measure.

And he walks with you now.

Service, in Mark 10:45, isn't weakness. It is identity revealed through love.

Prayer

Jesus, you chose the path of service freely and faithfully. When my own service feels heavy or unnoticed, remind me that you know this road. Guard my heart from bitterness or burnout. Teach me to serve in a way that reflects your love without losing myself. Amen.

Journaling Prompt

Where does your caregiving feel purposeful, and where does it feel like depletion? How might Christ's example help you distinguish between the two?

Caregiving shaped by Christ isn't about disappearing. It is about aligning your strength with love.

Considering Others First

*"Don't do anything for selfish purposes or out of pride,
but with humility think of others as better than yourselves.
Instead of each person watching out for their own good,
watch out for what is better for others."*

Philippians 2:3–4, CEB

Paul writes these words from prison. That changes how we hear them. He speaks as someone whose freedom has been taken, whose daily life is shaped by limits he did not choose. His call to humility isn't abstract theory. It rises from lived vulnerability.

Still, "think of others as better than yourselves" can feel unsettling to caregivers who already feel invisible or stretched thin. Read carelessly, it can sound like permission to erase yourself or accept harm quietly. But the humility Paul describes isn't self-contempt. It is a reorientation of attention.

Humility, here, isn't believing you matter less. It is refusing to let ego sit at the center.

Caregivers understand this instinctively. You arrange your day around someone else's needs. You notice signals others overlook. You make decisions that protect comfort or dignity, even when it costs you convenience. Not because your life has less value, but because love has trained your focus outward.

Yet Paul's words don't call you to neglect yourself. He doesn't say, "Ignore your own good." He says, "Don't watch only for your own good." There is a difference. Caregiving can become distorted when humility turns into silent self-abandonment. Christlike humility is discerning. It asks, What does love require here? Not, How do I disappear?

The verses that follow anchor everything in Christ. "Adopt the attitude that was in Christ Jesus." Humility flows from participation in his life. It is learned by walking with him, not by shaming yourself into smaller space.

Caregiving forms this mindset slowly. Over time, you become someone who notices others deeply. Someone who can step outside immediate self-interest and ask what serves love best. That isn't weakness. It is formation.

And formation is rarely visible from the outside. But God sees it.

Prayer

God, when I am tired, my attention shrinks to survival. Teach me humility that flows from love, not from self-erasure. Help me care for others without abandoning myself, and shape my heart to reflect the mind of Christ. Amen.

Journaling Prompt

Where do you sense a healthy outward focus in your caregiving, and where might humility need to include clearer boundaries for your own well-being?

Lower Than You Expect

*"So if I, your Lord and Teacher, have washed your feet,
you too must wash each other's feet. I have given you an
example—you should do just as I have done for you."*
John 13:14–15, CEB

In our time, foot washing feels symbolic. In Jesus' world, it was ordinary and necessary. Roads were dusty. Sandals were open. Feet were dirty. Washing them was the work of the lowest servant in the household, done quietly and close to the ground.

That is the work Jesus chooses.

And he chooses it deliberately. This happens on the night before his arrest. He knows what is coming. He knows who will betray him and who will deny him. With all of that pressing in, he kneels. He takes a towel. He touches what others would rather avoid.

The power of the scene isn't that he is forced low. It is that he goes low willingly.

Caregiving often occupies that same physical, unglamorous space. Bodies are fragile. Fluids spill. Schedules revolve around cleaning, lifting, adjusting, tending. These are not tasks most people imagine when they picture a meaningful life. They can feel humbling in ways that scrape at pride and patience alike.

Yet this is where Jesus places himself.

Foot washing is intimate. It requires closeness. It requires entering someone else's vulnerability without flinching. Peter recoils because the moment feels backwards. Leaders don't kneel. Teachers don't scrub grime from their students' feet. Jesus insists anyway.

But notice: he kneels from strength, not from shame.

Caregiving can sometimes feel like being pushed down by circumstance. That is different from choosing to love. Jesus' example isn't an endorsement of humiliation or silent suffering. It is a picture of love that is willing to move toward what is messy and embodied because another person needs care.

When you kneel beside a bed, when you clean, lift, steady, and tend, you are not performing something beneath you. You are practicing a love that stays close.

If caregiving has brought you lower to the ground than you expected, remember this: Christ has already been there. Not trapped there, but choosing that place as an expression of love.

Prayer

Jesus, you chose to kneel when you had every right to stand above. When my own caregiving feels humbling or uncomfortable, remind me that you are not absent from this space. Teach me to serve from strength, not shame, and to love without losing dignity. Amen.

Journaling Prompt

Where does caregiving feel like it has lowered you in ways that are painful? Where does it feel like a chosen expression of love? How can you tell the difference?

As If You Were Serving Me

"I assure you that when you have done it for one of the least of these brothers and sisters of mine, you have done it for me."

Matthew 25:40, CEB

Jesus speaks these words at the end of a long and sobering teaching. The scene he paints isn't sentimental. It is clarifying. People are surprised by what mattered and what did not. They are not asked to recite what they believed. They are asked how they responded to need.

The standard Jesus names is concrete: feeding, visiting, clothing, showing up. Ordinary acts directed toward people who could not repay them.

Caregivers hear this passage differently.

When Jesus says "the least of these," he isn't speaking in metaphor. He names people whose needs are visible, ongoing, and often inconvenient. People who require patience, time, and presence. People who depend on others.

But notice something essential. Jesus doesn't say, "Help them so that I will reward you." He says, "When you did it for them, you did it for me."

This is identification, not transaction.

He binds himself to the vulnerable. He so fully associates with those in need that serving them becomes an encounter with him.

That shifts the question entirely.

Much religious energy can go toward deciding who is right, who is wrong, who deserves correction. Even Scripture can be turned outward like a measuring stick. In Matthew 25, Jesus turns our attention toward mercy. Not performance. Not superiority. Attention.

The people who served in the parable did not realize they were serving Christ. They were not building spiritual resumes. They were simply responding to the person in front of them.

Caregiving lives in that same posture. You are not caring in order to earn standing with God. You are responding to real need. And Jesus says that in those quiet, repetitive acts, he is closer than you think.

This passage doesn't mean you must carry everything alone. It doesn't sanctify exhaustion. It does mean that the work you do in obscurity isn't spiritually insignificant.

If caregiving has narrowed your focus to one fragile life, don't assume your world has shrunk. According to Jesus, you are standing in a place where heaven and earth meet.

Prayer

Jesus, open my eyes to see you in the person before me. Guard my heart from turning service into performance. Teach me to respond to need with compassion, trusting that you are present in places the world overlooks. Amen.

Journaling Prompt

Where have you experienced caregiving not as obligation, but as an unexpected encounter with something sacred?

You are not caring in order to earn standing with God. You are responding to real need. And Jesus says that in those quiet, repetitive acts, he is closer than you think.

What the Lord Requires

"He has shown you, O mortal, what is good. And what does the Lord require of you? To act justly and to love mercy and to walk humbly with your God."

Micah 6:8, NIV

Micah speaks into a religious culture that is busy and sincere. The people are offering sacrifices. They are asking what God wants and how much is enough. Their instinct is familiar: if we perform the right rituals, we will be secure.

Micah redirects the question.

God doesn't ask for more spectacle or heavier religious performance. God names a way of life. Justice. Mercy. Humility. Not abstract virtues, but practices meant to shape the person who walks with Him.

That shift matters.

When we hear "what does the Lord require," we often think in terms of rules to enforce or standards to defend. Micah turns the focus toward formation. What kind of person are you becoming? How does your life reflect God's heart?

Caregiving lives inside that question.

To act justly, in caregiving, is rarely dramatic. It is advocating when someone else cannot. It is insisting on dignity in medical offices, classrooms, and care facilities. It is persistence when systems are slow or impersonal. Justice here isn't theory. It is phone calls, paperwork, and quiet refusal to let someone be overlooked.

To love mercy is to resist hardening. Caregiving exposes you to fatigue, disappointment, and grief. Mercy keeps your heart tender. It makes room for patience when irritation would be easier. It allows forgiveness when frustration builds. It includes compassion not only for the person you care for, but for yourself when you fall short.

And to walk humbly with your God is to recognize limits. You cannot control outcomes. You cannot solve every problem. You walk beside God, not ahead of Him. Humility here isn't shrinking yourself. It is remembering that you are not the savior of the story.

Micah pulls faith out of argument and into daily life. He doesn't ask what others should be doing. He asks how you will live.

If your faith has been shaped more by acts of care than by religious debate, you are already practicing what Micah describes. Justice. Mercy. Humility. Not perfectly, but faithfully.

This is what the Lord requires. And this is a road you know well.

Prayer

God, when faith feels complicated, return me to what is good. Teach me to practice justice with courage, mercy with tenderness, and humility with trust. Walk with me in the small, steady work of caring for others. Amen.

Journaling Prompt

Which part of Micah's call—acting justly, loving mercy, or walking humbly—feels strongest in your caregiving right now? Which one might need gentle attention?

Filled, Not Fixed

May the God of hope fill you with all joy and peace in believing, so that you will overflow with hope by the power of the Holy Spirit.

Romans 15:13

Paul writes these words near the end of a long letter addressed to a divided church. Tensions linger. Questions remain unresolved. His own future is uncertain. He doesn't pretend everything is settled. Instead, he anchors his blessing in who God is: "the God of hope."

And then he chooses a striking verb. Fill you.

Not fix you. Not immediately change your circumstances. Fill you.

That distinction matters for caregivers. Much of caregiving life is lived in the long middle—after the shock, before the resolution, in the steady repetition of responsibility. If hope depends on circumstances improving, it will thin quickly. But if hope is something God supplies, it can coexist with unfinished stories.

Paul ties hope to joy and peace "in believing." Not in understanding. Not in controlling. In believing. That word suggests ongoing trust, not tidy certainty. It is the decision, made repeatedly, to place your weight on God even when the ground feels uneven.

For caregivers, believing often looks quiet. You rise. You tend. You advocate. You return tomorrow. There may be no dramatic spiritual breakthrough. Just continued trust.

Notice also that hope overflows. It isn't scraped together from exhausted reserves. It comes "by the power of the Holy Spirit." This hope doesn't deny grief or fatigue. It flows alongside them. And because Paul writes to a community, not just an individual, it reminds us that hope is meant to spill outward—sustaining not only you, but those around you.

Hope in hardship rarely arrives as a surge of confidence. More often it arrives as sufficiency. Enough peace to steady your breathing. Enough joy to soften despair. Enough trust to take the next step.

The God of hope doesn't wait for everything to resolve before filling you. He meets you in the long middle.

Prayer

God of hope, when I feel worn thin, fill what I cannot refill on my own. Give me joy and peace that don't depend on quick answers. Let your Spirit steady me today and teach me to trust you in the unfinished places. Amen.

Journaling Prompt

Where are you living in an unfinished story right now? What would it mean to receive hope as a filling rather than something you must manufacture?

Through the Valley

Even when I walk through the darkest valley, I fear no danger because you are with me. Your rod and your staff— they protect me.

Psalm 23:4

Every caregiver knows something about dark valleys. Sometimes it is sudden—a diagnosis that redraws the future in a single conversation. Sometimes it is slow and chronic— the steady erosion of sleep, strength, and certainty. You keep walking because someone depends on you. That doesn't mean you are not afraid.

Psalm 23 doesn't promise a valley-free life. It assumes valleys are part of the journey.

What changes in this verse isn't the terrain, but the address. Earlier in the psalm, David speaks about the Lord. Here, he speaks directly to Him. "You are with me." In the valley, faith becomes personal. Less theory. More presence.

The rod and staff are not weapons aimed at the sheep. They are tools of care. The rod defends against threat. The staff guides, hooks, steadies, pulls back from ledges we cannot see. For caregivers navigating unfamiliar systems, frightening symptoms, and relentless uncertainty, that image matters. You are not left to calculate every step alone.

And then there is that quiet phrase: "I walk through."

The valley is real. The shadows are real. But they are not permanent residence. Walking through doesn't mean moving quickly. It may mean inching forward. It may mean walking with tears. It may mean pausing often. But it means you are not abandoned there.

God's presence doesn't erase darkness. It transforms isolation.

Caregiving valleys can feel lonely even when you are surrounded by activity. Psalm 23 whispers that you are accompanied. The Shepherd doesn't shout directions from a distance. He walks.

Prayer

Shepherd of my soul, you know the valleys I would never have chosen. When fear rises and the path feels narrow, remind me that you are not observing from afar. You are with me. Guard me when I feel vulnerable. Guide me when I cannot see clearly. Keep me moving, even if only one step at a time. Amen.

Journaling Prompt

Where does fear tend to rise most in your caregiving right now? What might it mean to speak to God directly in that place rather than only thinking about Him?

When the Outer Self Wears Down

So we aren't depressed. But even if our bodies are breaking down on the outside, the person that we are on the inside is being renewed every day. Our temporary minor problems are producing an eternal stockpile of glory for us that is beyond all comparison, because we don't focus on the things that can be seen but on the things that can't be seen. The things that can be seen are temporary, but the things that can't be seen are eternal.

2 Corinthians 4:16–18

Paul writes these words after years of strain. His relationship with Corinth has been bruising. He has been criticized, doubted, beaten, imprisoned, hungry, exhausted. When he speaks of the outer self wearing down, he isn't exaggerating. His body carries the evidence.

And still he says, "We aren't depressed." Not because suffering is small, but because it isn't ultimate.

Notice the plural. We. Renewal, for Paul, isn't a solitary achievement. It happens within a community that keeps trusting together. That matters for caregivers, who can feel alone in their fatigue.

The tension he names is familiar. The outer self weakens. The inner self is renewed daily. Not after recovery. Not once the crisis ends. Daily. Renewal runs parallel to strain.

Caregiving exposes the outer limits quickly. Bodies tire. Emotions thin. Decisions accumulate. The visible wear is undeniable. But Paul asks us to consider another layer of reality. Something unseen is being shaped: patience under pressure, compassion stretched wider than comfort, endurance that did not exist before.

Then come the words that can jar: "light and momentary." If they came from someone untouched by pain, they would sound hollow. But Paul is comparing, not dismissing. He places present suffering against eternity. Against what lasts. In that scale, even years of hardship don't get the final word.

The visible is loud because it is immediate. The unseen feels fragile because it requires trust. Paul chooses to anchor himself in what cannot yet be measured.

This isn't a call to deny exhaustion. It is permission to believe that exhaustion isn't all that is happening.

Your faithfulness isn't evaporating into thin air. The love you practice, the endurance you develop, the compassion you extend—these are not temporary traits. They are part of something that outlasts this season.

The outer self may be wearing thin. The inner life isn't wasted. It is being renewed in ways you cannot fully see yet.

Prayer

God, I feel the cost of this road in my body and spirit. Help me trust that you are doing more than I can measure. When the visible strain overwhelms me, steady my heart in what endures. Renew me today, even in the middle of weariness. Amen.

Journaling Prompt

Where is the visible strain most obvious in your life right now? What qualities might be forming quietly beneath that strain?

This isn't a call to deny exhaustion. It is permission to believe that exhaustion isn't all that is happening.

When Love Runs Thin

Above all, show sincere love to each other, because love brings about the forgiveness of many sins. Open your homes to each other without complaining. And serve each other according to the gift each person has received, as good managers of God's diverse gifts.

1 Peter 4:8–10

Peter writes these words to believers living under strain. Pressure was rising. The future felt uncertain. In that climate, small irritations could easily fracture relationships. So he begins simply: Above all, love.

At first glance, this sounds like church instruction. And it is. But caregiving is its own kind of intense community. When life is lived in close quarters—physically or emotionally—every weakness is magnified. Fatigue sharpens tone. Frustration rises faster. Affection can feel thinner than we want it to be.

Peter reminds us that love isn't a passing feeling. It is a steady decision.

"Love covers a multitude of sins." That doesn't mean ignoring harm or excusing injustice. It means refusing to let every misstep become a final verdict. In caregiving, tensions surface. Words are spoken too quickly. Reactions misfire.

Love steps in not to deny what happened, but to prevent it from hardening into resentment.

"Be hospitable without complaining." That line can sting when your home feels more like a medical hub than a sanctuary. Equipment arrives. Appointments rotate. Privacy shrinks. Yet hospitality here is less about entertaining and more about posture. It is choosing openness over bitterness, even when life feels crowded.

Then Peter adds something freeing: "Serve according to the gift each person has received." God's grace is diverse. Not identical. Not uniform. You are not required to be endlessly patient, relentlessly cheerful, medically knowledgeable, emotionally unshakable, and spiritually profound all at once.

You serve from the grace you have been given.

Some bring steadiness. Some bring humor. Some bring organization. Some bring quiet tenderness. You are a manager of grace, not its manufacturer.

When love feels worn thin, remember this: you are not drawing from a private reservoir. The Spirit who sustained Peter's weary congregation sustains you. Love can be renewed. Patience can be rebuilt. Grace can be replenished.

Not perfectly. But sufficiently.

Prayer

Father, when closeness magnifies my impatience and fatigue, renew my love. Guard my heart from resentment. Help me serve from the gifts You've given rather than from expectations I cannot meet. Teach me to practice grace without ignoring truth. Amen.

Journaling Prompt

Where has fatigue made love feel harder lately? What particular gift has God given you that can shape how you serve in this season?

Peace Even When Facing the Worst

Peace I leave with you; my peace I give you. I give to you not as the world gives. Don't be troubled or afraid.

John 14:27

John places these words in the final hours before Jesus' arrest. This isn't a calm devotional setting. It is a farewell spoken in a room thick with confusion and dread. Jesus knows what is about to unfold. The disciples don't. The peace he offers comes on the edge of chaos.

"I don't give as the world gives."

The world's version of peace is fragile. It depends on control, stability, favorable outcomes, and predictable futures. It is easily shaken because it rests on circumstances behaving themselves.

Jesus offers something different.

"My peace." Not distraction. Not denial. Not the promise that nothing will go wrong. His peace is the steady trust he himself lived with—the unbroken confidence in the Father's presence even when betrayal, arrest, and the cross were ahead.

Caregivers know how quickly external peace can unravel. You can follow every instruction, make every call, prepare for every contingency, and still watch the night fall apart.

Stability today guarantees nothing about tomorrow. If peace depends on things going well, it won't last long.

But Christ's peace isn't built on control. It is rooted in companionship.

When Jesus says, "Don't be troubled or afraid," he isn't scolding anxiety. He is inviting trust in the middle of it. His peace doesn't eliminate the storm. It steadies the heart within the storm. It meets you when medical updates shift, when exhaustion peaks, when you find yourself bracing for what might come next.

Circumstances may not calm down. But you are not left alone inside them.

Prayer

Father, the peace I try to build for myself is easily shaken. Teach me to receive the peace your Son gives—the kind rooted in your presence, not in perfect outcomes. When fear rises, anchor me in Christ's steadiness. Help me face what comes without being ruled by it. Amen.

Journaling Prompt

Where are you relying on controlled circumstances for peace right now? What might it look like to shift your trust toward Christ's presence instead?

He Wept

Jesus knew how the story would end.

He knew Lazarus would live again. He knew death wouldn't have the final word. Resurrection was not a distant theory to him. It was an act he was about to perform.

And still, standing at the tomb, Jesus wept.

That matters.

It tells us something essential about grief and about God. Foreknowledge doesn't cancel sorrow. Certainty doesn't silence love. Even divine power doesn't insulate the heart from loss.

Jesus did not weep because he lacked understanding. He wept because he was fully present. He stood beside Mary and Martha. He saw the faces of mourners. He felt the weight of death in a world he loved. John even hints that he was deeply disturbed, moved in spirit. Not only sad, but stirred. Death isn't natural to the kingdom of God. It is an intruder. And Jesus doesn't treat it lightly.

In that moment, God doesn't remain distant from human suffering. God, in flesh, feels it.

This is one of Scripture's most important revelations. God doesn't merely observe grief. God enters it.

For caregivers, that is a quiet relief. You may believe deeply in resurrection. You may trust that death doesn't win. And still, grief rises. Tears come. Faith doesn't erase sorrow, and Scripture never suggests it should.

Jesus' tears tell us that grief isn't weakness. It is love reacting to rupture.

Peace that "passes understanding" doesn't come from pretending loss is small. It comes from being accompanied in it. Knowledge alone doesn't comfort. Presence does.

When Jesus wept, he revealed a God who isn't impatient with sorrow, even sorrow that will one day be redeemed. He doesn't rush grief toward resolution. He meets it at the tomb.

If you are grieving today, know this: your tears are not corrected by hope, and they are not contradicted by faith. They are shared by a Savior who stood before resurrection power and still chose to weep.

Prayer

Jesus, thank you for meeting grief with tears instead of distance. When sorrow rises in me, help me trust that you are not disappointed or unmoved. Be present with me in the pain that knowledge cannot ease, and hold me until peace comes in ways I cannot explain. Amen.

Journaling Prompt

Where have you felt grief even while holding onto hope? How does knowing that Jesus wept shape the way you understand your own tears?

Comfort That Is Given, Not Assigned

Blessed be the God and Father of our Lord Jesus Christ,
the Father of mercies and the God of all comfort,
who comforts us in all our affliction,
so that we may be able to comfort those who are in any
affliction,
with the comfort with which we ourselves are comforted by
God.

2 Corinthians 1:3–4

Many caregivers have heard some version of this phrase: "There's always a purpose." It is usually spoken with kindness. Sometimes it brings reassurance. Other times it feels like pressure, as though suffering must be justified in order to be endured.

Paul doesn't move in that direction.

He doesn't explain affliction. He doesn't trace it back to a hidden design. He doesn't suggest that suffering is assigned for a lesson. He simply names it as real. "Affliction" is part of the human story.

What he names first is God.

The Father of mercies. The God of all comfort.

Comfort comes before explanation. Mercy comes before meaning-making.

Paul doesn't say God causes affliction so that something useful can grow from it. He says God meets us in it. God's first response to suffering isn't analysis. It is presence.

Sometimes, over time, something good does emerge from what was broken. But that doesn't mean the brokenness was necessary. It means that nothing falls outside the reach of God's mercy. As Maya Angelou said, "God doesn't waste pain." That is very different from saying God creates it. It means sorrow isn't beyond redemption, even when it is beyond understanding.

Only after comfort is received does Paul speak of comforting others. And even then, it isn't a command to hurry toward usefulness. It is a natural overflow. When you have been steadied in your own affliction, you may find yourself able to sit beside someone else without flinching. Not because you have answers, but because you know how to remain.

Caregivers often discover this quietly. You may not have explanations. You may not have tidy theology. What you have is patience. A listening presence. A refusal to rush grief. That kind of comfort isn't manufactured. It is learned in being comforted.

If you are in the middle of affliction right now, let this passage speak its first word to you. God isn't demanding that you extract purpose from pain. God isn't asking you to make suffering acceptable.

God is offering mercy. God is offering comfort. Right here.

Prayer

God of mercy, I am weary of trying to explain what hurts. Thank you for being the God who comforts rather than justifies. Meet me in my affliction with your presence. Help me receive your mercy without feeling the need to make sense of everything. Amen.

Journaling Prompt

When you think about your suffering, do you feel pressure to explain it? What would it mean to rest instead in God's comfort without resolving every question?

Hope That Keeps You From the Rocks

We have this hope as an anchor for the soul. It is secure and firm.

Hebrews 6:19

In 1889, warships from several nations crowded into Apia Harbor, Samoa. Political tension kept them anchored there longer than was wise. When a powerful cyclone swept in, the harbor that once seemed safe became deadly. Wind tore through the narrow waters. Ships dragged anchor. Chains snapped. One vessel after another was driven toward reefs hidden by darkness and spray.

From the deck of HMS *Calliope*, the British captain watched the chaos unfold. He knew he could not stop the storm. The only question was whether his ship could hold long enough to survive the night.

An anchor cannot silence wind or flatten waves. It cannot promise rescue. What it can do is hold position. It buys time. It keeps a vessel from being smashed against the rocks while the storm does what storms do.

This is the kind of hope Hebrews describes.

An "anchor for the soul" doesn't eliminate hardship. It steadies you within it. In Hebrews, this hope is rooted in

God's unbreakable promise and in Christ who has gone before us. It isn't optimism. It is attachment to something firmer than circumstance.

Anchors work below the surface. You don't see them doing their work. You know they are holding because the ship remains.

Caregivers understand this kind of hope. The waves don't stop. Diagnoses don't reverse on command. Exhaustion doesn't evaporate. But something deeper holds. You are not drifting as far as you might have. You are not breaking apart as completely as the pressure suggests you should.

Hope, in this sense, isn't emotional brightness. It is stability.

Hebrews doesn't ask you to become the anchor through determination. It reminds you that you already have one. This hope is given. It holds when strength thins. It keeps you through long nights when morning is still invisible.

The storm may rage. The anchor remains.

Prayer

God, when everything feels unstable, remind me that my hope rests in you, not in calmer weather. Hold me steady when I feel pulled in every direction. Anchor my soul in your promises and keep me through this night. Amen.

Journaling Prompt

Where do you most feel the strain of the storm right now? In what quiet ways has hope been holding you in place, even when you barely noticed it?

When Hope Is Forged

*But not only that! We even take pride in our problems,
because we know that trouble produces endurance,
endurance produces character, and character produces hope.
This hope doesn't put us to shame, because God's love has
been poured out in our hearts through the Holy Spirit, who
has been given to us.*

Romans 5:3–5

At first glance, Paul's words can feel jarring. "Take pride
in our problems"? That can sound like celebration of suffering. But Paul isn't praising pain. He is expressing confidence
in what God can shape within it.

He describes a progression.

Trouble produces endurance. Endurance produces character. Character produces hope.

Hope doesn't come first. That order matters.

Caregivers often feel they need hope in order to endure.
Paul suggests something different. Endurance begins in the
unglamorous repetition of showing up. You tend. You decide.
You advocate. You adjust. Not because you feel inspired, but
because someone needs you.

Over time, that endurance forms character. It shapes
steadiness. It clarifies what matters. It strips away illusions

94

about control. You become someone who can remain when remaining is difficult.

And then hope begins to take root.

Not the hope of quick solutions. Not the hope that everything will reverse. But a tested hope. A hope that has survived nights you didn't think you could get through. A hope that has looked disappointment in the face and kept breathing.

Paul says this hope "doesn't put us to shame." It doesn't collapse under pressure. Why? Because its foundation isn't endurance itself. Its foundation is love.

God's love has already been poured out.

That is the climax of the passage. The chain doesn't end in human resilience. It ends in divine generosity. The Spirit pours love into hearts that would otherwise run dry.

Caregiving can strip away romantic ideas about faith. What remains is something more honest. Hope becomes less about what might change and more about who remains faithful. You discover that endurance was never the final goal. It was the soil in which hope could grow.

And beneath it all is love — not your love alone, but God's love holding you from within.

Prayer

God, I don't boast in hardship, but I long for hope that holds. When endurance feels heavy, remind me that your love has already been poured into my heart. Shape in me a hope that has been tested and steadied by your presence. Amen.

Journaling Prompt

Where has endurance already changed you? How has God's love sustained you in ways you may not have recognized at the time?

Hope becomes less about what might change and more about who remains faithful. You discover that endurance was never the final goal. It was the soil in which hope could grow.

Real Peace, Real Love

Conduct yourselves with all humility, gentleness, and patience. Accept each other with love, and make an effort to preserve the unity of the Spirit with the peace that ties you together.

Ephesians 4:2–3

Paul writes these words to a church made up of very different people. Different histories. Different assumptions. Different temperaments. Unity did not mean sameness. It meant learning to live together in love despite those differences.

That isn't far from life in a caregiving household.

Caregiving places strain on everyone involved—the one giving care, the one receiving it, and the ones orbiting around both. Stress magnifies differences. Fatigue sharpens tone. Small misunderstandings can swell quickly. Peace can feel fragile.

Paul doesn't pretend unity happens naturally. He says, "Make every effort." Guard it. Protect it. Preserve it.

Notice, though, that he calls it "the unity of the Spirit." The unity isn't something we invent. It is something the Spirit has already woven. Our task isn't to create it from scratch, but to keep from tearing what God has joined.

Humility makes space. It lowers defenses long enough to listen. Gentleness slows reactions that would otherwise escalate. Patience absorbs friction without snapping.

These are not personality traits. They are practices.

"The peace that ties you together" isn't the absence of disagreement. It is the presence of a bond strong enough to survive it. In caregiving, that bond is tested regularly. Exhaustion can make everyone more brittle. Plans unravel. Roles blur. Emotions run close to the surface.

Harmony doesn't come from pretending everything is fine. It comes from returning—again and again—to love. From remembering why you are bound together in the first place. From choosing to protect the tie rather than prove a point.

Caregiving will strain every strand of that tie. But the Spirit who binds hearts is stronger than the pressures that pull them.

Prayer

Father, when stress threatens our unity, remind me that your Spirit has already tied us together. Give me humility to listen, gentleness to respond, and patience to endure tension without tearing the bond of peace. Help me protect what you have joined. Amen.

Journaling Prompt

Where does unity feel most strained in your caregiving relationships right now? What would "making every effort" look like in that specific place?

Not the End of the Story

He will wipe every tear from their eyes.
Death will be no more.
Mourning and crying and pain will be no more,
for the former things have passed away.

Revelation 21:4

This verse is often read as comfort, and it is. But it is future comfort, not present correction.

Revelation doesn't say tears are unnecessary now. It doesn't tell us that mourning is misplaced or that pain should resolve quickly. It names them plainly. Tears exist. Death exists. Grief exists. They are heavy enough that Scripture must promise their end.

What makes this vision powerful isn't that suffering is minimized, but that it is finished. Not reinterpreted. Not justified. Not spiritualized. Ended.

And notice who wipes the tears.

God doesn't issue a decree from a distance. God doesn't command tears to stop. God draws close and wipes them away. The image is intimate. Personal. It assumes tears have been shed and treats them as worthy of tender attention.

For caregivers, this matters. Many aches don't resolve neatly. Some losses linger for years. Even after faithfulness.

Even after long seasons of care. Revelation doesn't ask you to deny that reality. It places your grief inside a larger story.

This promise isn't only personal. It is cosmic. Death itself will be undone. Pain won't merely be managed; it will be removed. The "former things" will pass away, not because they were insignificant, but because they will no longer define existence.

Christian hope isn't the belief that everything will someday make sense. Some things may never feel reasonable. Our hope is that what breaks our hearts now won't have the final word.

The promise isn't that you will look back and approve of every loss. The promise is that God is moving history toward a day when suffering truly ends.

Until then, we live in between. Between tears and their wiping. Between death and its undoing. Between grief and glory.

Revelation doesn't rush you forward. It simply assures you that the story isn't finished.

Prayer

God, I long for the day when death and pain are no more. Until then, help me live faithfully in the space between sorrow and promise. Hold my tears now, and anchor my hope in the future you have prepared. Amen.

Journaling Prompt

Which part of this promise feels distant to you right now? Where does it quietly steady you, even if only a little?

A Little Sugar in the Cup

"Rejoice always. Pray continually. Give thanks in every situation because this is God's will for you in Christ Jesus."
1 Thessalonians 5:16–18

On the surface, Paul's words can feel unrealistic. Rejoice always? Give thanks in every situation? For caregivers, some days are built more for endurance than celebration.

But notice what Paul does and doesn't say. He doesn't say, "Be grateful for everything." He says, "Give thanks in every situation." The difference isn't small.

Caregiving can be exhausting, tangled, and emotionally complicated. There isn't thing holy about pretending it is easy. Gratitude here isn't denial. It is direction.

I've learned something simple: if I can find one honest reason for gratitude inside a hard day, it shifts something in me.

It doesn't remove the bitterness. But it sweetens it slightly, like a spoonful of sugar in strong coffee. The coffee is still strong. The day is still demanding. But the taste changes.

Maybe the gratitude is small. A nurse who listens carefully. A moment of unexpected calm. The strength to finish a difficult task. Even the stubborn love that keeps you showing up.

That one thread of thanksgiving keeps frustration from hardening into resentment.

Paul himself knew suffering. He wrote to the Thessalonians as someone acquainted with prison cells, beatings, and rejection. When he says "rejoice" and "give thanks," he isn't speaking from comfort. Gratitude, for him, was not circumstantial. It was relational. It was anchored in belonging to Christ.

Rejoicing, praying, and giving thanks flow together. Gratitude keeps prayer from becoming only desperation. Prayer keeps rejoicing from becoming denial. Together, they form a steady rhythm in unstable circumstances.

Giving thanks in every situation isn't emotional performance. It is choosing to notice that mercy and hardship can coexist.

Sometimes that choice is as small as asking: What is one thing, right now, that I can honestly thank God for?

The situation may not change. But you may.

Prayer

Father, some days I struggle to see anything beyond fatigue. Open my eyes to the mercies that coexist with difficulty. Teach me to give thanks honestly, not artificially, and let gratitude steady my heart in the middle of what feels heavy. Amen.

Journaling Prompt

What is one specific, genuine reason for gratitude in your caregiving today? How does naming it reshape your heart, even slightly?

Entering with Thanksgiving

"Enter his gates with thanks; enter his courtyards with praise! Thank him! Bless his name!"

Psalm 100:4

Psalm 100 is a pilgrimage song. It imagines worshipers walking toward the temple, nearing the gates, stepping into the courtyards. And it tells them how to enter.

Not once everything is resolved.
Not after life settles down.
With thanksgiving.

That order matters.

Thanksgiving isn't something saved for the inside. It is the way in. Gratitude becomes the doorway into God's presence.

For caregivers, that can feel unrealistic. Many days don't resemble a bright courtyard. They look like another appointment, another difficult conversation, another long stretch of responsibility. Yet the psalm suggests that gratitude isn't the result of ideal conditions. It is the posture we carry as we step into them.

This kind of gratitude isn't denial. It is orientation.

When I focus only on what is draining, the day contracts. When I pause to name even one mercy, my perspective widens. The situation may not change, but I remember that I am not entering it alone.

Jesus gave thanks before multiplying loaves that seemed insufficient. He gave thanks before breaking bread on the night of betrayal. Gratitude preceded provision and preceded suffering. It was not based on ease. It was rooted in trust.

Psalm 100 reminds us that thanksgiving doesn't inform God of anything new. It clarifies something in us. It re-centers us in God's goodness before the day begins to pull at us from every direction.

When you enter a caregiving day with even quiet thanksgiving, you are saying: God is already here. This space, however ordinary or exhausting, isn't outside His presence.

That doesn't erase fatigue. It changes how you carry it.

Sometimes the only thanksgiving available is small. Thank you for this breath. Thank you for strength for one more task. Thank you that love still moves me to show up.

That is enough. Gratitude opens the gate.

You may not control what waits inside the courtyard. But you can choose how you enter.

Prayer

Father, as I step into today's responsibilities, help me enter with thanksgiving. Not because everything is easy, but because You are present. Let gratitude orient my heart toward You before the demands of the day take hold. Amen.

Journaling Prompt

What small, specific thanksgiving could become your doorway as you step into tomorrow's caregiving responsibilities?

When Songs Stay Inside You

"The word of Christ must live in you richly. Teach and warn each other with all wisdom by singing psalms, hymns, and spiritual songs. Sing to God with gratitude in your hearts."

Colossians 3:16

Paul writes these words to believers who are not living easy lives. Following Christ in the first century often meant pressure, loss, and vulnerability. And yet Paul tells them to let the word of Christ dwell in them so fully that it turns into song.

Not performance. Not forced cheer. Song.

There's something deeply practical about that.

Songs stay with us. They repeat. They settle into memory. They rise uninvited in quiet moments. Paul seems to suggest that when Christ's word lives in us richly, it begins to take melodic shape. Truth becomes something we carry, not merely something we recall.

And melody reaches places plain words sometimes cannot.

Acts 16 gives us a vivid picture. Paul and Silas are beaten, stripped, and locked in stocks. It isn't poetic suffering. It is humiliating and painful. And at midnight, they are praying and singing hymns.

106

They are not singing because prison is pleasant. They are singing because worship has become part of who they are. The song doesn't depend on the cell door opening. It rises before the earthquake comes.

Caregiving can feel like its own kind of confinement at times. The walls are routines, responsibilities, and the narrowing of life around one person's needs. There are days when your body aches and your spirit feels thin.

This is where Colossians 3:16 matters.

Letting the word of Christ dwell richly isn't about emotional intensity. It is about saturation over time. Scripture learned slowly. Hymns sung repeatedly. Truth absorbed until it becomes instinctive. Over years, gratitude begins to hum beneath the surface.

You may not sing loudly. You may not sing out loud at all. But a remembered lyric during a long drive. A hymn that surfaces while washing dishes. A quiet line of Scripture whispered in the dark. These are not small things.

Song doesn't erase hardship. It refuses to let hardship have the final word.

For caregivers, that quiet resistance matters. Worship becomes less about Sunday performance and more about steady belonging. A melody that says, even here, even now, I am not alone.

Songs of gratitude don't deny exhaustion. They carry us through it.

And sometimes, that is enough.

Prayer

Father, when I am tired and words feel heavy, let Your truth rise in me like a song. Saturate my heart with Your Word until gratitude hums beneath the surface of ordinary moments. Teach me to carry melodies of trust that outlast my fatigue. Amen.

Journaling Prompt

What song, hymn, or line of Scripture has stayed with you through difficult seasons? How might letting it dwell in you reshape a weary moment this week?

Joy That Cannot Be Taken

"You have sorrow now; but I will see you again, and your hearts will be glad, and no one will take away your joy."
John 16:22

Jesus speaks these words on the night before his crucifixion.

That matters.

He isn't addressing people in comfort. He is preparing his disciples for confusion, fear, and apparent loss. "You have sorrow now," he says plainly. There is no denial. No softening. Sorrow is real, and it is coming quickly.

But then comes the promise: "No one will take away your joy."

He doesn't promise the absence of sorrow. He doesn't promise quick resolution. He doesn't promise understanding.

He promises a joy that survives.

Caregiving exposes how fragile ordinary happiness can be. A stable morning can unravel by afternoon. A hopeful report can be followed by a setback. If joy depends on smooth circumstances, it will always be at risk.

But the joy Jesus describes isn't built on conditions. It is built on relationship. "I will see you again," he says. Their joy will come not from the removal of pain, but from his presence after it.

After the resurrection, the disciples were not suddenly placed in easy lives. They still faced danger. They still suffered. But something irreversible had happened. They had seen the risen Christ. Death had been confronted and defeated. That reality did not erase sorrow, but it redefined it.

Caregivers often live in long stretches of uncertainty. Outcomes may not align with your hopes. Circumstances may not resolve the way you pray they will. But this promise isn't tied to outcomes. It is tied to Christ.

Joy, in this sense, isn't cheerfulness. It is steadiness. It is the deep assurance that you are not abandoned, that love is still at work, that this moment—however heavy—isn't ultimate.

Paul knew that kind of joy. Writing from prison, facing possible execution, he spoke of rejoicing. Not because chains were pleasant, but because Christ was present.

That is the joy Jesus offers. Rooted so deeply in God's faithfulness that it cannot be confiscated by diagnosis, fatigue, or fear.

You may have sorrow now. Jesus never denies that.

But sorrow doesn't have the authority to take everything from you.

There is a joy beneath it.

And no one can take it away.

Prayer

Lord Jesus, some days sorrow feels close and heavy. Anchor my heart in your presence rather than in my circumstances. When hardship presses in, remind me that your joy runs deeper than what I see and cannot be taken from me. Amen.

Journaling Prompt

Where does your sense of joy tend to rise and fall with circumstances? What might it look like to root your joy more firmly in Christ's presence rather than in outcomes?

When You Don't Know What to Do

But anyone who needs wisdom should ask God, whose very nature is to give to everyone without a second thought, without keeping score. Wisdom will certainly be given to those who ask.

James 1:5

Caregiving brings moments when love isn't enough. You need wisdom.

Do we pursue this treatment or stop it?
Is this symptom urgent or watchful waiting?
Am I pushing too hard, or not hard enough?
Is it time for more help?

These are not abstract questions. They carry consequences. They affect bodies, futures, and hearts. And often, you don't feel wise. You feel tired. Pressed. Afraid of getting it wrong.

James doesn't rebuke that feeling. He assumes it. "If anyone needs wisdom…" Of course you do.

James writes these words in the context of trials. He knows that testing exposes our limits. Wisdom isn't automatic. It isn't stored up in advance for future crises. It is needed again and again.

What makes this verse remarkable isn't just the invitation to ask. It is the character of the One who gives.

God gives without hesitation.
Without keeping score.
Without shaming you for needing to ask again.

Caregivers ask again. Circumstances change. New variables appear. What was right last month may not be right today. You may find yourself praying the same request for guidance repeatedly.

James says you are not a burden when you do that.

God's generosity isn't reluctant. It is intrinsic to who He is. He doesn't say, "You should know this by now." He doesn't ration wisdom to the spiritually advanced. He gives to those who ask.

That doesn't mean wisdom always arrives dramatically. Often it unfolds quietly. A conversation that brings clarity. A growing sense of peace about one path over another. A check in your spirit to slow down. A door that opens—or one that closes. Wisdom can look ordinary and still be divinely given.

It is also not the same as guaranteed outcomes. You can make the wisest decision available and still face hardship. James isn't promising control. He is promising guidance sufficient for this moment.

Caregiver, you are allowed not to know.

You are allowed to ask.

You are allowed to say, "God, I need help thinking clearly."

And the promise stands: wisdom will be given.

Not because you are flawless.
Not because you are calm.
But because God is generous.

Prayer

God, I feel the weight of decisions I never imagined I would have to make. I don't want to act from fear or exhaustion. Give me wisdom. Steady my mind, clarify my judgment, and guide me toward what is loving and faithful. Thank you for giving generously and without shame. Amen.

Journaling Prompt

What decision feels most pressing right now? What would it look like to ask God specifically—and repeatedly— for wisdom in that area?

Help From Higher Ground

I raise my eyes toward the mountains.
Where will my help come from?
My help comes from the Lord,
the maker of heaven and earth.

Psalm 121:1–2

We live in the foothills of the Great Smoky Mountains. As I write this, we have just come back from a few days up there, driving winding roads, stopping at overlooks, taking in views that make you catch your breath. Layer upon layer of blue ridges fading into the distance.

The mountains are beautiful.

But beauty isn't the whole story.

We passed houses built along steep drops, their back decks stretching out over open air. I remember thinking, "What a view." And then, almost immediately, "You would have to be very careful there." Toss a ball for the dog without watching, and it could disappear into a ravine. Take the trash out at night without paying attention, and one misstep could carry you somewhere you never meant to go.

Mountains are breathtaking. They are also unforgiving.

Psalm 121 begins with that kind of realism. "I raise my eyes toward the mountains. Where will my help come from?" The psalmist isn't admiring scenery. He is looking at

115

terrain that demands caution. The road ahead is steep. The footing uncertain.

Caregiving can feel like that. There is fierce beauty in love. And there are edges. One missed dose. One overlooked symptom. One decision made in exhaustion. The stakes feel high. The drop-offs close.

So the question is honest: Where will my help come from?

Not from constant vigilance alone.
Not from perfect decisions.
Not from my ability to foresee every hazard.

"My help comes from the Lord, the maker of heaven and earth."

That line widens everything. The One who shaped mountains and carved valleys isn't intimidated by their edges. The God who made heaven and earth isn't surprised by the steepness of your road.

The psalm goes on to say that this God watches over you. He doesn't slumber. He keeps your coming and going, now and forever.

The mountains don't disappear. The cliffs don't flatten. But you are not walking them alone.

Sometimes help looks like strength to slow down. Sometimes it is wisdom to ask for support. Sometimes it is the quiet steadiness that keeps panic from taking over when the terrain shifts.

Lifting your eyes isn't denial of danger. It is perspective. The mountain is real. But it isn't ultimate.

Caregiver, the edges may feel close right now. The view may be beautiful and terrifying at the same time. But your help doesn't rest on your ability to manage every cliff. It comes from the Lord, maker of heaven and earth, who sees the whole landscape and watches over every step.

Prayer

God, the road before me feels steep, and the edges sometimes feel too near. Lift my eyes beyond what frightens me to your steady presence. Watch over my steps. Keep me when I feel unsure of my footing. Be my help on this high ground. Amen.

Journaling Prompt

Where do you feel most aware of the "edges" in your caregiving right now? What would it mean to trust that God is watching over your steps, even when you cannot see the whole path?

A Final Word

By now, you know that caregiving is not a straight road.

It bends. It stretches. It asks more of you than you expected.

And still, here you are.

Showing up.
Doing what needs to be done.
Finding strength where you can.

There will be days when you feel steady, and days when you don't. Days when faith feels close, and days when it feels distant.

All of it belongs.

As you go forward from here, you don't need to carry everything at once. Take what you need for today. Leave the rest for another time.

And when the storm feels strong again, come back to what anchors you.

You are not alone in this.

Topic Guide

(Finding a Devotional for the Moment You're In, title followed by page number)

When You Feel...

Overwhelmed or like everything is collapsing
— *When the World Falls Apart 1*
— *Through the Valley 77*

Exhausted and worn down
— *Strength for the Weary 39*
— *When the Outer Self Wears Down 79*

Afraid or uncertain about what's ahead
— *Never Alone in the Battle 13*
— *Held When You Feel Unsteady 24*

Alone, even when others are around
— *Always With You 17*
— *The Lord Is Close 15*

Grief that won't settle or keeps returning
— *Bound, Not Rushed 51*
— *He Wept 87*

Frustrated, restless, or stuck in a season you didn't choose

Confused about why this path is yours

Anxious, with thoughts that won't slow down

Discouraged or close to giving up

When You Need...

Strength to keep going

Peace in the middle of chaos

Hope that actually holds

Wisdom for decisions you're not sure how to make

When You Are Facing...

About the Author

Donn is an emeritus professor of communication studies at Pellissippi State Community College in Knoxville, Tennessee, and a pastor in the United Methodist Church, as well as a speaker, writer, and communication coach.

He writes posts and books that challenge, encourage, and equip people to live in courageous alignment with their values. He also works with independent authors who want to publish with confidence so they can avoid the DIY frustration, release books they're proud of, and focus on writing..

He has spoken to audiences, churches, and radio audiences across the United States and written numerous newspaper, magazine, and blog articles, along with his primary work of writing books and hosting The Alignment Show. His books and his podcast help people live their values to value their lives.

For over 40 years, Donn has taught college students and business leaders the skills of effective communication. In recent years, he has guided dozens of professional speakers, teachers, and presenters in the effective use of Zoom for engaging communication. He is the winner of the Excellence Award and the Innovation Award, both from the National Institute for Staff and Organizational Development.

He earned a B.A. in communications from Freed-Hardeman University in Henderson, Tennessee, and an M.S. in communications from the University of Tennessee, Knoxville.

Donn is married to Janet. Together they have five children, three of whom are grown and independent, and two of whom have passed away. Donn and Janet live on the quiet side of the Great Smoky Mountains, where Donn teaches and writes, and Janet makes amazing creations from yarn, and where they enjoy the best coffee in Tennessee.

Also by Donn King

The Right-brained Guide to Parliamentary Procedure: A Path Through the Wilderness

Responsibly Spoken: A Manual for Public Speaking and Business and Professional Speaking

Creating While Caring: Practical Tips to Keep Creating While Caring for a Loved One

The Sparklight Chronicles

The Way of the Three-Year-Old Why: Live What Really Matters

Medium Well: The Journey from Believing to Believing In

Acknowledgments

This book didn't come together in a season. It grew out of more than twenty years of living, learning, and caring. I can't name everyone who shaped it, but I want to name a few who stood close enough to leave fingerprints on these pages.

Rev. Catherine Nance, who stood with us when our oldest son died, and again when the one for whom we had cared for so long passed away. Thank you for your steady presence, your friendship, and your willingness to enter hard moments with us rather than stand at a distance.

Rev. Ann Robins, pastor, mentor, and friend, who helped shape both my ministry and my understanding of what it means to walk with people faithfully over time.

Jim Stovall, friend, mentor, colleague, and spiritual brother. Thank you for your encouragement as a writer and for modeling the depth and power that devotional writing can carry.

Leslie Price Martinich, who provided a professional eye in proofreading these pages. You spotted things that make it better, and I appreciate that for all those supported by these pages.

John David Mann, author and mentor extraordinaire, but your support, encouragement, and insight into all the many layers of professional writing.

To the many **nurses**, **doctors**, and **caregivers** who cared for Hannah and, just as importantly, cared for us along the way—thank you for your skill, your patience, and your compassion.

To my wife, **Janet**, who has walked this entire road with me. We were given more than we expected and more than we would have chosen, and you bore it with quiet strength and deep love. You carried your own burdens while standing with me in caring for Hannah, and the cost of that cannot be measured. I am grateful beyond words for your partnership, your endurance, and your love.

www.ingramcontent.com/pod-product-compliance
Lightning Source LLC
Chambersburg PA
CBHW051457050726
47593CB00005B/2106